THE
WORKING POOR:
TOWARDS A
STATE AGENDA

The Council of State Planning Agencies is a membership organization comprised of the planning and policy staff of the nation's governors. Through its Washington office, the Council provides assistance to individual states on a wide spectrum of policy matters. The Council also performs policy and technical research on both state and national issues. The Council was formed in 1966; it became affiliated with The National Governors' Association in 1975.

In addition to *Studies in State Development Policy,* the Council publishes:

■ *CSPA Working Papers.* Current volumes address: environmental protection and economic development; commercial bank financing for small business enterprise; the investment of public pension funds; venture capital and urban development; the impact of regional shopping malls; the operation of minority capital markets; and the public service costs of alternative development patterns. A full list of current volumes is available on request.

■ *State Planning Issues.* A journal concerning the problems and practice of planning in the states. Published twice yearly.

■ *The State Planning Series.* Sixteen short papers dealing with financial management, citizen participation, econometrics, urban and rural development, policy development techniques, multi-state organizations, federal-state partnerships, and other issues of concern to state officials.

To order *Studies in State Development Policy* see page 91.

The Council of State Planning Agencies
Hall of the States
444 North Capitol Street
Washington, D.C. 20001
(202) 624-5386

Robert N. Wise
Director

Michael Barker
Associate Director for
Community and Economic Development

C-417

THE WORKING POOR: TOWARDS A STATE AGENDA

DAVID M. GORDON

COVER: "Map 1963," by Jasper Johns. Collection Albert Saalsfield. Grateful acknowledgement is made to Mr. Johns for allowing the reproduction of his work.

Partial funding support for this volume was received from the Office of Economic Research, Economic Development Administration, the U.S. Department of Commerce. The views and findings it contains are the author's, and do not necessarily represent those of the Economic Development Administration or the members or staff of The Council of State Planning Agencies. Reproduction of any part of this volume is permitted for any purpose of the United States Government.

Library of Congress Catalog Number: 79-67382

ISBN: 0-93482-03-5

Printed in the United States of America. First printing - 1979.

Format conceptualization and series coordination: Katherine Kinsella
Design: Kathy Jungjohann
Typesetting and Layout: Teri Grimwood
Printing and binding services: George Banta Co.

ACKNOWLEDGEMENTS

This essay was made possible by a grant from the Council of State Planning Agencies to the Institute for Labor Education and Research. The views expressed here are the author's and do not reflect those of either the Institute for Labor Education and Research or the Council of State Planning Agencies.

I would like to express my appreciation for research help from David Howell, for typing help in a pinch from Linda Long, and for hospitality and amusement from everyone else at the Institute for Labor Education and Research. I am most grateful to Michael Barker of the Council of State Planning Agencies, who steadily funneled materials in my direction, cajoled this essay into its final shape, and displayed a stoic's patience at the repeated delays in its completion. Despite all that help, I have nonetheless blundered in many places— for which I absolve my colleagues of any intellectual (or political!) responsibility.

TABLE OF CONTENTS

INTRODUCTION

"We have to tell a state considering additional restrictions on business: 'The next plant doesn't go up here if that bill passes.'"

—a corporate executive at a recent management conference (quoted in Silk and Vogel, 1976: 66).

State governments are currently facing a wide variety of serious employment problems. Wages are low and many state residents are unable to make ends meet. At least in some regions, jobs are scarce and unemployment rates are high. Occupational health-and-safety problems are attracting increasing attention and, in many respects, getting worse. And management/labor relations have been seriously strained in many areas over union prerogatives and right-to-work initiatives.

These problems are confronting State governments with particular urgency, in part, because other levels of government within the federal system will not or cannot place priority on employment problems. At the federal level, both the recent Republican administration and the current Democratic administration have explicitly sacrificed employment programs for the sake of anti-inflationary policies. At the local level, the fragmentation of metropolitan governments has meant that city administrations cannot easily mobilize either the revenues or the political leverage to confront employment problems in their areas. State governments are left with a critical public responsibility for employment problems and their potential moderation.*

Many State governments have adopted a common approach to this responsibility, often identified as an "economic development strategy." The approach begins with essential reliance on private business for solutions to current employment problems, hoping to support business efforts through some combination of public programs—such as tax relief, development subsidies, and supportive training programs. There is every indication that this approach is spreading, that it represents much more than a temporary reflex reaction to the first signs of the "tax revolt" and "Proposition 13 fever." According to

---

*Throughout this essay I have adopted the convention of capitalizing the word "State" in order to clarify my continuing reference to the problems and policies of State governmental units within the federal system.

1

a comprehensive 50 state survey by the *New York Times* in the summer of 1979, "farmers, manufacturers and other business interests around the country have been granted state tax relief on a scale unknown in recent years . . . " (Herbers, 1979). This relief has not been an inadvertent by-product of the citizens' revolt against taxes, the *Times* survey concludes:

> The relief extended to business interests stemmed in part from the emphasis that is being placed on private economic development, both by government officials and other leaders throughout the country . . . [In addition to middle class taxpayers] the state actions were . . . intended to benefit . . . commercial interests that have long maintained powerful lobbies in state capitals and have capitalized on middle class protest.

Many State government officials justify this approach to economic development on either or both of two grounds—(1) that tax relief and business subsidies will actually help generate jobs and reduce employment problems; and (2) that there are no other alternatives to public support for private business in the employment area.

This essay disputes that policy orientation. It argues that State government relief and subsidies for private business will not reduce and may even intensify many State employment problems. It also argues that other approaches, centered around public support for and management of non-profit, locally controlled community economic development programs, are possible and hold much greater promise for moderation and eventual solution of current employment problems. It argues, in short, that a careful analysis of State employment problems suggests the need for a dramatic re-orientation of State government policies toward economic development.

This argument is developed in four steps:

■ Chapter 1 reviews the character and magnitude of employment problems in the United States. Its major conclusion is that recent public discussion has largely misperceived the nature of those problems. The economy does not simply need *more* jobs, no matter what working and living conditions they provide. *The economy needs more "good jobs,"** and that requirement should frame discussions of State employment policies.

---

*Throughout this essay I continually refer to "good jobs" with quotation marks in order to indicate that the phrase requires definition and that the notion of "good jobs" is not a concept about which there is common agreement. Chapter 1 provides a provisional definition of "good jobs" and Chapter 2 a more rigorous one.

■ Chapter 2 reviews explanations of current employment problems, focusing particularly on why the economy does not generate enough "good jobs." The discussion compares two quite different answers to that question: (a) the mainstream economic analysis which has shaped and helps justify the current strategy of tax-and-subsidy support for private business; and (b) an alternative structural analysis which, in my view, both provides a better explanation of the sources of current problems and helps reveal the reasons for the inadequacy of more traditional analysis.

■ Chapter 3 discusses the implications of that analysis for policy approaches to current employment problems, focusing on how State governments could, in general, help generate more "good jobs" in the economy. The chapter argues that the distinction between the mainstream and alternative analyses discussed in Chapter 2 translates into a distinction between what can be called "traditional" and "community" approaches to the solution of current employment problems. The "traditional" approach builds upon a faith that support of private business will *also* improve the working and living conditions of the vast majority of State residents. The "community" approach, drawing on an alternative economic analysis, suggests that there may actually be a conflict between support for private business and concern for the welfare of most State workers and residents.

■ Chapter 4 applies that discussion of general policy approaches to a review of specific policy tools which State governments currently apply or which are potentially available for the State government policy arsenal. Using earlier arguments about the sources of employment problems, the chapter distinguishes between "promising" and "unpromising" uses of policy instruments. If State governments want to help promote a much larger supply of "good jobs," the chapter suggests, they will need to consider a wide variety of new policy directions in their employment and development programs.

The arguments advanced in these chapters directly challenge the conventional wisdom. I have no illusions that these kinds of policy changes can happen immediately or that they would come easily if suggested. Viewed in that perspective, this essay seeks nothing more than a discussion based on common sense. I think that current employment policy is based on misperceptions of the problems and a misguided analysis of their sources. Policies based on that analysis are likely, if anything, to make our problems worse. It seems to make much more sense to move in promising (though difficult) directions than to pursue policies which are more likely to intensify than to solve the problems they are supposed to address.   *3*

1
CURRENT EMPLOYMENT PROBLEMS: NOT ENOUGH "GOOD JOBS"

State residents confront a wide variety of serious employment problems in the United States. The mix of problems varies among states and regions. Despite the multi-dimensional and regionally varied character of current employment problems, however, a common thread runs through all of the most important problems throughout the country: The U.S. economy needs millions more "good jobs."

This chapter develops that argument in two sections. The first section reviews the current character and magnitude of the four main employment problems confronting State residents: *poverty, unemployment and underemployment, indecent working conditions,* and *inadequate job control.* The second section argues that all of those problems flow from a common source—not enough "good jobs." The section provides both a definition of "good jobs" and a summary of the implications of this view of employment problems for the objectives of State economic development policy.

THE MAJOR DIMENSIONS OF STATE EMPLOYMENT PROBLEMS

This section argues that the four main dimensions of employment problems require urgent attention, are not going away (and, in several cases, clearly getting worse), and are not confined to any specific region in the country.

Poverty

Since the belated discovery of the poor in the early 1960s, the federal government has encouraged the public to consider poverty as a residual and dissolving problem. The government and most economists have defined poverty as a marginal problem which economic growth was gradually eliminating. Many if not most State governments have followed suit.

In fact, as even government studies admit, official federal poverty standards are inadequate.[1] The official Social Security Administration (SSA) poverty level income builds upon the estimated costs of a minimal necessary food basket. But as the original studies formulating **5** that budget standard noted, the food standard was based upon prospective diets for people seeking to survive in bomb shelters during civil emergencies, a nutritional diet designed only for "temporary and emergency use." No one ever intended that diet as the basis for regular subsistence; according to nutritional studies, health problems would soon result if people tried to subsist at that dietary level for more than a few months, let alone many years.

And still, the federal government persists in considering households as poor *only if* their incomes are too low to afford food consumption at this "temporary or emergency" level. Judging by these standards, the government and many experts have noted the virtual disappearance of poverty in the United States. Federal data suggest that the percent of the U.S. population living in "poor" households has declined from 22.1 percent in 1960 to only 11.8 percent in 1977. By 1977, "only" 25 million Americans lived in poverty.

If this official federal poverty standard seems inadequate, are there other definitions of poverty which might more effectively reflect the real dimensions of poverty in the country and among States?

Many economists have suggested applying another federal budget standard as a more adequate and realistic "poverty" standard—the "lower-than-moderate" budget standard developed and updated by the U.S. Bureau of Labor Statistics. Although higher than the SSA Standard, it provides a spare existence. For instance, each adult in the family is allowed two beers a week in the food budget. The entertainment budget permits each adult five movies a year. Families earning incomes lower than this standard, as many economists have argued, have trouble sustaining their families at minimal levels of nutritional health and well-being. The federal government does not directly tabulate the number of households who remain poor by this definition. The author has elsewhere estimated that roughly *30 percent* of Americans live in households which, by this more meaningful standard, should be considered "poor" (Gordon, 1977: Ch. 4). With nearly a third of Americans falling below this budget standard, it is difficult to consider poverty a "marginal" problem.

Is poverty a regional or national problem? Historically, because wages have always been lower in the South, the incidence of poverty has been higher in the Sunbelt than in the Northeastern States. In 1960, for example, poverty (measured by the SSA standard) was twice as high in the South as in the West, North, or North Central regions of the United States.

Another historic pattern, particularly since World War Two, has also been that poor Southerners tended to migrate to the North in large numbers, providing a safety valve to Southern poverty and, at least eventually, increasing Northern burdens for welfare expenditures and social services. Even after the net flow of total migration shifted back from North to South during the 1960s, it appeared that the net flow of *poor* migration was continuing to move northward—that, as a Census observer recently put it, the South "was continuing to contribute, on an annual basis, to poverty levels elsewhere" (Long, 1978).

But this historic pattern has now shifted. Since 1970, there has been a net *in*-migration of poor people to the South (and the net in-migration of poor people to the West has continued). As economic opportunities have expanded in the Sunbelt, poor people have been staying in the South rather than searching for steady income elsewhere. The incidence of poverty in the South has continued to decline, but much more slowly. Recent data indicate that the Sunbelt and the Frostbelt will become more and more similar along this dimension. (See Pack, 1978.)

It is important to note, finally, that poverty by either standard is *not* principally a problem of those who cannot work—the elderly or disabled or single parents without access to day care facilities. In the early 1970s, even according to the SSA poverty standard, a majority of all poor people lived in households where the head worked at least some weeks during the year; a quarter of the poor lived in households where the head worked year-round (Plotnick and Skidmore, 1975). Measuring by the BLS "lower-than-moderate" budget standard, the heads of nearly a third of poor households in 1975 worked *full-time and year-round*. Only about one-fifth of the poor (as measured by the BLS standard) lived in households where the head did not work at all (Gordon, 1977).

In short, millions of U.S. households earn too little to support themselves at a minimally adequate standard of living and a substantial majority of those households—as high a fraction as four-fifths—remain in poverty despite the fact that the households' heads worked at some time or another during the year.[2] This means that, for most of the poor in the United States, their poverty does not arise because they cannot find work or are incapable of holding a job. Rather, their poverty continues despite the fact that they work repeatedly and often steadily. Correcting their poverty would require, therefore, higher wages on the jobs they hold, not more jobs at prevailing wage levels.[3]

Unemployment and Underemployment   The second dimension of State employment problems has received the most attention in recent discussions of regional **7**

decline and growth. The media seem to suggest that *unemployment* has become an essentially regional problem, concentrated in the "declining" Northeast. But these impressions are somewhat misplaced. They reflect much too partial a view of the problem of "unemployment." When we consider the issue more broadly as an issue of jobs—of "employment" itself—then we begin to see that there are severe problems of unemployment *and* underemployment throughout the country. The main difference between regions lies in the *form* in which these general problems *manifest* themselves.

What is the general problem? In the U.S. economy, most people are not able to support themselves (at adequate incomes) for long unless they can find stable and decent employment. This means that the basic problem of employment, unemployment, and underemployment has a simple definition. People have "employment problems" when they are unable to secure a steady job which pays an adequate wage or salary. Some people experience this "problem" in the form of unsteady employment. Others experience it in the form of inadequate wage or salary. Many experience the problem in both forms. In any case, unemployment rates—as most economists now admit—measure only part of this nexus of problems.

The conventional government definition of unemployment includes only those people without a job *who have looked for a job during the past four weeks.* This means that a wide variety of people with "employment problems" are not counted in the unemployment rates: (1) those who would like to work but have grown discouraged from their search and have stopped looking, (2) those who want full-time work, cannot find it, and have settled for part-time work; (3) those who work full-time but earn inadequate labor incomes; (4) those who might be looking for jobs in the civilian labor market but who, for largely economic reasons, are settled elsewhere—in prisons, for example, or in the armed forces; and (5) those whom the census takers never locate.

As with the problem of poverty, the federal government has consistently failed to compile data which would fully measure this broader conception of what many economists now call "underemployment." Some approximate estimates of the problem have been developed, however, incorporating various definitions of critical concepts like "adequate" wage-and-salary income and "discouraged" workers (Gordon, 1977). In 1975—the most recent year for which complete data were available at the time of calculation—the "official" unemployment rate was 8.5 percent. By the most conservative combination of definitions of "underemployment," a minimum of 16 million people—or 17 percent of the labor force—suffered employment problems. By more liberal definitions—including the spare BLS "lower-than-moderate" budget standard as the basis for "adequate" wage-and-salary income—roughly 35 million workers—or 33.8 percent of the labor force—were "underemployed."

In other words, at a minimum, twice as many workers suffer employment problems as the official unemployment data suggest. More plausibly, something like four times the official unemployment rate experience basic employment problems. By the more inclusive definitions, roughly a third of the labor force is unable to secure a job providing adequate wage-and-salary support.

These figures don't even account for the "steadiness" of those jobs. All employment data, including the expanded figures for under-employment discussed above, measure such problems *at one time.* They do not provide estimates of the number of people, for example, who experience unemployment *at one time or another during a year.* Roughly two and a half times as many people experience *at least one bout of unemployment* during a year as those counted as unemployed at any time during the year. Indeed, so severe are the problems of steady employment in the United States, particularly during the current period, that only two-thirds of all workers are able to work *full-time year-round.*

In short, somewhere from a third to a half of all U.S. workers suffer employment problems of one sort or another. These problems are not simply confined to central city ghettos in declining States.

Nonetheless, there are important differences in the character of those employment problems among States and regions.

In the Northeast, one of the most important problems has been rising relative unemployment rates. Compared to the national average, the official rates of unemployment in the Northeastern States have been increasing steadily since the late 1960s. This has meant that national economic growth has been less and less likely to generate additional employment opportunities for those living in the Frostbelt region.

In the Sunbelt, in contrast, the major problem remains one of low wages. Throughout the Sunbelt region, many jobs pay wages which are far too low to support workers and their households at adequate income levels. Although aggregate per capita income in the Sunbelt has been increasing more rapidly than in the Frostbelt during the recent period of regional shift, it remains true that much of the Sunbelt employment generated during the region's recent prosperity has not afforded employment at decent wages for much of the Sunbelt labor force.

In both regions, despite these differences, the basic problems are similar. Even in the Sunbelt states, unemployment rates are often very **9**

Photo: Earl Dotter/ALEC

high. In 1977, for example, when the national "official" unemployment rate was 7.0 percent, Alabama, Arizona, California, Florida, Mississippi, and South Carolina all had unemployment rates above the national average. Even in the Frostbelt, where average wages have been higher, millions of jobs pay far too little for adequate household support. In 1977, for example, 36 percent of all households in the ten largest Northeast and Midwest central cities earned less than $10,000—the level required for a family of four to achieve the BLS poverty standard.

It is important to emphasize, moreover, that simply expanding a State's employment base does not provide full protection against the problems of unemployment and underemployment. Many jobs typically provide *unsteady* employment, jobs in which workers are particularly likely to suffer dismissal or layoff. Many of the same kinds of jobs also typically provide such low wages that they do not establish a foundation for households' maintaining an adequate standard of living. A large number of studies have recently shown that very high proportions of workers suffering frequent bouts of unemployment and of those earning inadequate wages are concentrated in a group of what we can call "secondary" or "poor jobs." (See below for definitions; see also Edwards, 1979; and Gordon, 1980a, for a summary of recent studies.)*

Does unemployment and underemployment really matter? Isn't it possible for State government officials to remain content with expanding employment and to pay less attention to the quality of the jobs which workers find and hold? Why should State economic policy focus on the third to half of jobs which fail to provide steady employment at decent wages rather than the seven percent of the labor force which is unemployed at any given moment?

Many economists have pointed out that high unemployment rates and unstable employment opportunities impose heavy social service costs on State and local governments—not only through public support of the unemployment compensation system but through higher relative welfare and social service costs. These costs of high unemployment and low wages seem fairly obvious.

There are some more subtle and possibly more important social costs of underemployment. Crime offers one of the most important examples. High and rising crime not only imposes property losses on local residents but also creates an acute sense of public insecurity and

---

*Throughout this essay I refer to "poor jobs" as the opposite of "good jobs" and requiring similar definition. The definition emerges from the definition of "good jobs" later in this chapter and then again in Chapter 2.

social malaise. Crimes are not solely or even primarily committed by marginalized citizens—by roving bands of professional criminals. Recent economic evidence suggests that crime varies directly and closely with two critical economic variables—unemployment and inequality. As unemployment rises, so does crime. And as the gap between the incomes of the wealthy and the relatively poor increases, so do crime rates rise. The largest proportion of those who commit "street crimes" are people who occasionally work in "secondary" jobs, who suffer frequent bouts of unemployment, and whose wages at work are inadequate to support their families (McGahey, 1979).

These direct effects spill over between the generations. Problems of underemployment among parents contribute to feelings of frustration and low expectations among children. Those communities in which underemployment rates are high tend also to be those in which a variety of social problems persist among teenagers into young adulthood. The quality of schooling suffers, which infects future opportunities for children who themselves come from families supported by steady jobs. The consequences of underemployment spread throughout such communities like ripples in a pond (see Gordon, 1975).

The problems of unemployment and underemployment, in short, cannot be marginalized. Millions of U.S. workers are unable to find steady jobs at decent wages. This underemployment creates severe problems not only for those workers directly affected but also for many others in neighboring communities.

Indecent Working Conditions

Another dimension of State employment problems has only recently received serious attention. Many jobs expose workers to treacherous hazards, including the risk of fatal accidents or potentially fatal diseases. Since the passage of the Occupational Safety and Health Act of 1970, working people have been complaining more and more frequently about these basic hazards. And their complaints have finally begun to highlight the enormity of the problem.

Conservative government estimates suggest that between 115,000 and 200,000 Americans die each year from an occupationally related accident or disease. At least two million workers suffer occupational accidents every year; some government studies have suggested that so many accidents or diseases go unreported that closer to 20 million U.S. workers suffer some kind of occupationally related accident or disease *each year*. Recent studies have suggested that at least one in four U.S. workers is exposed to working conditions which increase their risks of potentially fatal disease.[4]

12   Many media reports on occupational health-and-safety problems

have tended to view the sites of this exposure as confined to limited pockets in specific industries—like the mining or the textile industries. Obviously, however, it would be difficult to draw a map of the U.S. in such a way that one out of four workers (exposed to potentially fatal working conditions) were isolated in a few pockets of dangerous industrial areas.

Comprehensive data on the geographic incidence of health-and-safety problems are difficult to muster and interpret. One reasonable index of the geographic distribution of problems can emerge from cancer mortality figures. Most studies conclude that from two-thirds to three-fourths of all cancers are environmentally caused and that large proportions of those cancers result from on-the-job exposure. The variation of cancer mortality among States therefore provides an interesting glimpse at the varying intensity among States of dangerous working conditions on the job.

13

Data for cancer mortality among States for 1969 reveal a common pattern. States with the traditionally highest concentration of manufacturing industry and population have the highest cancer mortality rates: New Jersey, Rhode Island, New York, and Connecticut, for example, were the four States with the highest rates in that year. This common pattern suggests an obvious implication for the Sunbelt states. As industry shifts to the South and West and as population density also increases, there is a strong likelihood that cancer mortality rates will increase as well. Sunshine may be the best disinfectant, as Justice Brandeis once remarked, but no one has yet shown it to provide a cure for cancer.

Many health-and-safety problems are also concentrated disproportionately in "poor jobs." Industrial accident rates are highest in some industries like mining and construction where the character of the work is especially likely to expose workers to physical hazards. But it turns out that accident rates are *also* highest in industries where high competition and low profit rates mean that firms rely on outmoded technology, cannot afford improvements and maintenance, and must drive their workers unusually rapidly to try to keep up their profits. If we compare accident rates among manufacturing industries in the 1960s and 1970s, for example, we find that accident rates in what economists sometimes call "peripheral" industries average roughly twice as high as those in "core" industries. (See Chapter 2 for definitions.) (Health problems deriving from carcinogenic substances are much more widespread throughout industry.)

Health-and-safety problems are not disappearing, moreover, but have intensified since economic instability began to intensify during the late 1960s. Industrial accident rates increased by 27 percent between 1963 and 1970 after years of decline. During the 1970s, based on new and more comprehensive data collected under the auspices of the Occupational Safety and Health Administration, workdays lost from industrial accidents increased by one-third, on average, between 1971-73 and 1975-77.

Job Control

Many workers also face serious employment problems because they have relatively little control over their working conditions, exposing them to the risks of employer negligence or mistreatment. A variety of employment problems can sometimes flow from this common source: The less influence workers have over the pace and organization of work, the more vulnerable they may be to health-and-safety problems. The less protection workers have against arbitrary dismissal and supervisory abuse, the more difficulties they may have with sudden layoffs and intermittent employment.

These concerns have fueled workers' historic drive to win the right to unionization. During the 1930s, according to most labor historians, workers participating in the drive to form industrial unions were at least as concerned with supervisory abuse—leading to demands for grievance procedures—and arbitrary hiring and promotion—leading to proposals for seniority systems—as they were with more tangible issues like wage rates. (For example, see Bernstein, 1971: p. 774 ff.) These concerns also obviously motivate more recent union support for strong government regulation of health-and-safety hazards.

One measure of trends in workers' influence over their working conditions, therefore, focuses on trends in unionization. The evidence here suggests a very clear tendency. The percentage of the non-agricultural labor force represented by labor unions increased steadily during the 1930s and 1940s. It peaked at roughly 35 percent in the early 1950s and has since fallen to roughly one quarter. In many Western European countries, by contrast, the percentage of the labor force in unions ranges from half to more than two-thirds. While labor union membership is hardly sufficient to provide workers with substantial influence over their jobs, it is nonetheless much more difficult for workers to improve their working conditions *without* the protection and leverage which labor unions help afford. Why has there been such a striking decline in relative union representation?

Business leaders often argue that declining proportions of workers

Photo: Earl Dotter/ALEC

want to join unions because unions fail to serve their interests. Union leaders typically argue that millions of additional workers would join unions if there were not so many obstacles in their paths and if companies opposed unions less insistently.

There is certainly some truth on both sides. Several observations seem to support the union argument. First, the relative decline in union strength coincides historically with the period since the 1947 passage of the Taft-Hartley Act, which dramatically increased firms' ability to resist unionization and reduced the tools with which unions could seek to organize workers. Second, there is plentiful evidence that current legislation does not fully guarantee workers' rights to unionize, since companies can and frequently do delay elections and contract negotiations for years through stalling and legal challenges. Third, recent surveys indicate that roughly a third of workers not currently represented by labor unions would prefer to join and be represented by unions.[5]

Some other observations provide at least partial support to the business argument: Unions have become increasingly likely to lose decertification elections during the 1970s, for example, indicating that significant portions of workers have been willing to express their dissatisfaction with their current union's practices. Second, recent surveys also indicate that large portions of current union members are only moderately satisfied, at best, with their unions' performance.

There is a composite interpretation which probably more accurately reflects recent historical experience than either the business or union arguments. It seems reasonable to conclude that very large portions of U.S. workers want a significant degree of influence over their working conditions *but* that many are not currently satisfied with the manner in which some labor unions help provide such influence *and* that business opposition to union and worker influence, in many quarters, also substantially increases the obstacles to workers' influence (much less union representation and effectiveness). Is there evidence on worker preferences for influence over their working conditions? The same recent surveys indicate that more than 90 percent of U.S. workers want at least "some say" over wage determination, conditions affecting job security, and decisions affecting health-and-safety conditions. It seems reasonable to conclude that the recent relative decline in union strength and the aggressive business promotion of its own interests have *not* been increasing workers' ability to realize these preferences.

It is important to note, finally, that this problem of worker influence is not simply a regional problem, confined to those areas, particularly in the Sunbelt, where workers have traditionally faced the greatest difficulty in organizing unions. It is true that rates of unionization differ substantially between the Frostbelt and the Sunbelt. In 1974, for example, more than 30 percent of the (non-agricultural) labor force was unionized in most of the Northeastern states, while from seven to 17 percent of the labor force in the Sunbelt states was unionized. But it is also reasonably clear that the issue of worker influence over working conditions affects State economic policymakers throughout the country. As firms have tended increasingly both to move away from the Frostbelt areas of the country (both to the Sunbelt and overseas) and as many companies have moved more and more aggressively to combat union influence, workers and State government officials in even the more pro-union states have experienced substantial pressure to grant more privileges and concessions to business in their areas. This has begun to have two important effects. First, even unionized workers are feeling growing pressure to relax their demands for greater job security and safer working conditions. Second, the "demonstration effect" of unions has probably been weakening. While it has historically been true—and most business observers would agree with this observation—that union successes in unionized sectors have pushed non-union employers to improve wages, job security and working conditions in order to try to forestall unionization, it seems likely that the recent decline in union strength and the recent increase in corporate aggressiveness have moderated this pressure on non-union employers—particularly in traditional union areas like the Northeast.

These two effects combine to generate a common result: Almost all workers in the United States want some effective influence over their wages, job security, and working conditions, but recent developments have tended to push that objective further and further from their grasp.

SO WHAT'S A "GOOD JOB"?

All four of these main dimensions of current employment problems reflect a common denominator: *The U.S. economy provides too few "good jobs."* Problems of poverty, underemployment, indecent working conditions, and inadequate job control all reflect this underlying problem.

Simple employment is not enough. As Eli Ginzberg, a noted manpower economist, has concluded (Ginzberg, 1977) "most specialists would agree that the following [job] characteristics are significant: wages, fringe benefits, regularity (or intermittency) of employment, working conditions, job security and opportunities for promotion." As Ginzberg also concludes, "more often than not, . . . favorable elements go together." A "good job" is one which provides, **17** therefore, *adequate wages and fringe benefits, job security and stable employment, decent working conditions, and opportunities for both advancement and control.*

I shall provide estimates of the number of "good" and "poor" jobs in the U.S. economy after I derive a method for more precise definition in Chapter 2. In the meantime, it is important to review and clarify the argument about the importance of "good jobs" for State employment policies.

One of the arguments about the importance of "good jobs" can be stated simply: *Simple job expansion by itself will not guarantee solution to any of the four main dimensions of State employment problems:*

■ If job expansion creates "poor jobs," poverty is unlikely to moderate significantly, since large numbers of the poor already work in "poor jobs." Indeed, recent estimates indicate that 92 percent of a representative sample of households who had received welfare over a five-year period had household heads who had worked at some time or another during that period (Harrison; 1979). The problem lay in the quality of jobs they held, not in the presence or absence of work itself.
■ If job expansion creates "poor jobs," the real problems of unemployment and underemployment are unlikely to abate more than marginally. Growing numbers of economists agree that many workers move in and out of "poor jobs" with great frequency—suffering layoff, dismissal, or disappointment in their hopes for stable employment with potential advancement. While we might reasonably expect that measured "official" unemployment rates might decline if the aggregate rate of "poor job" expansion increased, it is not at all clear that the numbers of people who experienced unemployment at some time or another during the year would decline or that the rate of *under*employment would be affected to any significant degree.
■ If job expansion merely increases the number of "poor jobs," there is a significant likelihood that workers' exposure to unsafe and possibly injurious working conditions would *increase* dramatically. "Poor jobs" are not only much more likely to manifest health-and-safety problems but they are also much more likely to expose workers to the problems of stress and anxiety which flow from intermittent employment and arbitrary supervisory authority (Luft, 1978).
■ Job expansion does not necessarily provide improved opportunities for advancement and job control. If the number of "poor jobs" increases, the problems flowing from inadequate control may increase correspondingly. (See Chapter 2 for elaboration of this point.)

18   There is another argument about the importance of "good jobs"

which reflects the *indirect* consequences of the quality of work: Simple job expansion by itself may do nothing to moderate (and may actually intensify) some of the most serious *social* problems currently plaguing State and local governments:

■ A wide variety of studies have shown that people who receive welfare benefits and commit "street crimes" often work in "poor jobs." Indeed, it appears that welfare and crime incidence increases with the gap between the incomes and working conditions of "good" and "poor" jobs—rather than increasing with higher unemployment by itself. The more that the U.S. labor market confines certain groups of people to "poor jobs" and seems to preclude their entry into "good jobs," the more the economy will reinforce the circulation of many people among the labor market, welfare, and street crime in a kind of continuous flow (Harrison, 1974, 1979).

Photo: Robert Gumpert

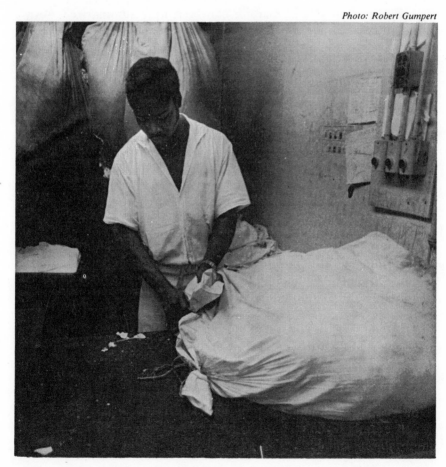

19

■ These arguments can be extended to even more generalized observations. Many note declining work satisfaction among U.S. workers and a growing cynicism about the country and its prospects. If job expansion does not provide growing proportions of the labor force with "good jobs," then we must certainly accept the possibility that labor market developments will do nothing to counter these trends toward dissatisfaction and cynicism. Charles Wilson used to argue that "what is good for General Motors is good for the country." One might suggest a more plausible maxim: "What is good for people's jobs is good for the country." The more that people can enjoy decent wages, job security, decent working conditions, and job control, the more likely they will be to contribute positively to the country's political economic welfare. The greater the numbers of people who are confined to "poor jobs," the greater the risks to our general welfare and the strength of the social fabric.

The argument of this chapter can be simply summarized. As we review State employment problems, it appears that we must define those problems somewhat more carefully than is common in general public discussion. It appears that *the moderation of State employment problems requires more "good jobs," not simply more jobs of whatever quality and characteristics.* This suggests that we must pose a very specific question for further discussion. Why does the U.S. economy fail to generate enough "good jobs"?

Footnotes to Chapter 1

1. On the inadequacies of the federal poverty definitions, see Levine (1970) and Rainwater (1975).

2. It is important to emphasize once again that almost all the data upon which these kinds of conclusions depend revolve around the federal (SSA) poverty standard. Despite all the inadequacies of that definition, the federal government does not provide data which would permit accurate conclusions about the relationship among welfare, poverty, and employment. Without such data, many of these conclusions remain approximate.

3. For a useful summary of the indications that poverty has not, in fact, been reduced and that it remains a critical and sizable problem, see National Advisory Council on Economic Opportunity (1979).

4. For basic references to data sources and summaries of these magnitudes, with appropriate discussion of the definitions on which they rely, see Ashford (1976) and Berman (1979).

5. These observations on workers' preferences about unions and working conditions all derive from Institute for Social Research (1979).

2

WHY AREN'T THERE ENOUGH "GOOD JOBS"?

Recent discussions of State economic development problems have typically pointed toward strategies of support for private investment and job expansion. These strategies flow not only from business pressure but from an underlying assumption—that market pressures and adequate corporate profit levels will promote the kinds of aggregate and regional growth necessary for the moderation of employment problems. The pervasiveness of the current "economic development strategy" derives in part from the prevalence and uncontested acceptance of these assumptions.

The foundation for these common viewpoints lies in mainstream (or "neoclassical") economic analysis. In order to ask why the economy does not provide enough "good jobs," we must obviously explore mainstream analyses of employment and income. This chapter reviews the predominant mainstream analyses of jobs and wages and compares those views with an alternative "structural" explanation of employment problems. Four main points are developed in the course of this review:

■ Mainstream economic analysis provides an inadequate account of labor market behavior, fundamentally compromising the policy recommendations which depend on it.
■ In particular, it provides a misleading set of answers to our questions about why the economy fails to provide enough "good jobs."
■ An alternative structural perspective appears to provide a much more promising account of labor market mechanisms and the determination of wages and employment.
■ In particular, this structural perspective seems to offer a coherent and consistent explanation of the economy's insufficient supply of "good jobs."

MAINSTREAM ECONOMIC ANALYSIS   Neoclassical economists typically burst with confidence about their explanatory powers. But recent events have tempered that self-confidence.

Many State and local officials have asked some obvious questions, for example, about the causes of rapid regional employment shifts and   **21** the relative decline of the Northeast. There are pieces of analysis which might potentially help, according to many mainstream economists, but there is no consistent underlying framework which fits all those pieces together. Two leading regional economists introduced a recent book of essays on *Revitalizing the Northeast* with exactly this kind of warning. Constructing a coherent theory of regional growth and decline, they admitted, "severely taxes present theoretical capacities as well as empirical resources . . . [There] is little we can do but be cognizant of this limitation and make it explicit" (Sternlieb and Hughes, 1978).

If this kind of hesitation is so pervasive, why are so many economists nonetheless confident about the kind of "economic development strategy" which dominates recent public discussions? I would argue that the underlying *tools* of mainstream economics provide the basis for recent policy formulations and that economists' continuing confidence in those basic tools frames their support for specific economic development strategies. In order to reconsider the basis of current policy perspectives, we must briefly reconsider the fundamental analytic perspective of neoclassical economics itself.[1] Two main aspects of that perspective warrant primary attention—its focus on "supply and demand" and its focus on workers' "productivities."

Traditional Supply and Demand Analysis

The starting point for most traditional economic analysis is the classic supply-and-demand framework. This set of ideas begins with some simple premises: In market economies, buyers and sellers adjust their demand and supply until they agree on a common price and quantity for the goods and services involved. Once they agree, an exchange takes place. The logic of the process is supposed to guarantee a stable "equilibrium," or resting place, for the exchange process. If we assume that there are available supplies of resources and prevailing "tastes" or preferences, then we can assume that the economy will keep reproducing the same basic structures of allocation and exchange over time.

This framework, in general, has an obvious implication about the sources of change in market economies. Since a market equilibrium will be continually reproduced with *given* resources and tastes, changes in the basic pattern of allocation must be caused by changes in basic *resources* and/or *tastes:* nothing would change if there weren't changes in what the market began with in the first place. This suggests that important economic changes must be due to significant shifts in the underlying conditions of supply and demand, not in the market processes themselves.

What does all this have to do with analyses of State employment problems or regional decline and growth?

Many analyses of current State economic problems begin with the basic supply and demand framework. They assume that there was some moment in the recent past when State and regional economies were in equilibrium, when buyers and sellers in factor markets and buyers and sellers of final goods and services were content with the terms of their exchange. The accelerating changes in State and regional fortunes, this framework suggests, *must* be the result of some underlying shifts in the conditions affecting the supply and demand of factors of production and goods and services.

The examples of this kind of analysis seem fairly obvious:

■ Many current problems are attributed to basic shifts in people's *preferences about where they live.* Much of the shift to the Sunbelt has been explained by a rapid movement in population for reasons of climatic preference. Once population began to shift, according to this argument, jobs began to follow. Nothing internal to the economy changed at all. The economy simply made accommodations to the change in people's preferences about residential location and older people's growing capacity to satisfy those preferences.

■ Many analyses also place a strong emphasis on *energy constraints.* Particularly since 1973-74, the costs of energy have been increasing rapidly. Climatic conditions tend to create different energy costs by region, and some historic differences in transportation patterns compound these variations in energy costs. Industry has been moving to the Sunbelt in growing numbers, the analysis concludes, because it can no longer afford the relatively higher energy costs of Frostbelt production. Nothing changed in the way the economy works, but changes in the technical conditions of energy resource production and distribution generated significant changes in market outcomes.

Not in real terms

■ Business decisions about location also depend heavily on other conditions affecting their supply curves, economists argue, like basic *wage* costs. If industry has been moving to other regions where wages are lower, the supply and demand perspective suggests that it must be happening at least in part because wages have been rising "too rapidly" in the regions from which capital has been fleeing. Nothing about the economy has changed, once again, but some external changes in the power of workers and their unions to increase their wages has unsettled the traditional spatial equilibrium and driven business away.

The character of this supply and demand analysis helps explain why it *appears* to many economists that there is no coherent analysis of the **23** dynamics of regional decline and growth. Within that general analytic framework, *any* change in underlying conditions—no matter how large or small, long-term or temporary—has equal credentials as a source of changes in market equilibria. And none of the changes is necessarily connected to any others. Each of the factors, as the authors quoted above also admit, is seen as a "discrete factor" in isolation from every other factor. The analysis seems more like a patchwork quilt than a structured analytic framework. Nothing matters more or less than anything else.

There are two main theoretical problems with this supply-and-demand framework. First, it assumes that everything can matter, and all changes in any conditions are equally likely to have some important effects in causing serious employment problems. In this sense, the analysis is very *undiscriminating,* failing to distinguish between different kinds of causes or different orders of importance. If something small happens—like small changes in workers' wages—the analysis assumes that those small changes are sufficient to bring about continuing and structurally important changes in economic conditions.

At first blush, this seems to be a plausible assumption. When we investigate its implications more carefully, however, it seems inherently implausible. It suggests that economic resources are organized in a sufficiently flexible manner, that firms can always and automatically make necessary marginal adjustments in resource allocation and production. But the real economic world involves significant structural *rigidities.* Firms can't change to a new location if there is no transportation, no infrastructure, no marketing mechanism, no stable governmental support for their needs, no regular accommodation with workers and labor unions. Just as a bee sting may not phase a hippopotamus, small changes in the costs and markets affecting firm decisions may not have *any* immediate impact simply because they are dwarfed by the more fundamental determinants of business activity. Structural rigidities, in short, may preclude small changes in the business environment from having much influence on basic paths of economic development no matter how "real" or "important" those small changes may seem. (This will have critical implications, as we shall soon see, for analyses of "economic development strategies" like reduced business taxes.)

The second main theoretical problem with the supply-and-demand framework is that it depends on the notion that the market is automatically self-correcting, that problems and inefficiencies in the economy will work themselves out smoothly. In neoclassical economic theory, this notion depends on several critical assumptions: (a) that

Photo: Robert Gumpert

economic markets are very competitive (and that firms cannot affect their economic environment); (2) that everyone in the markets has more or less *perfect* and *immediate* information about all alternative exchange possibilities; and (3) that buyers and sellers have more or less equal power to affect market outcomes.

But none of these assumptions makes much sense as a starting-point for analyses of the modern U.S. economy. (1) The largest corporations can clearly exercise significant influence over their environments; few markets are "perfectly competitive." (2) Information is very spotty and imperfect, with some insiders not only getting it more quickly than others but also actively hiding it from their competitors and potential market partners. (3) Market transactions typically involve buyers and sellers of very uneven and unequal power—large firms and small firms, large corporations and individual workers, firms and consumers.

If, indeed, these three assumptions make little sense, we cannot easily assume that the market has generally been in "balance" or "equilibrium" and that important changes have emanated from factors outside of the market framework. It would be just as plausible to assume that the economy was constantly in a state of "imperfection" and change, that large and powerful economic forces and actors, like corporations, are always trying to achieve differential advantage through manipulation of market exchange, and that they are frequently capable of achieving these kinds of results. Their activities **25** and influence, rather than "external" events, might easily explain many of current employment problems.

None of this means that supply-and-demand factors never matter. It suggests, rather, that the supply-and-demand framework builds from such misleading assumptions that we should never assume it is the *only* useful perspective for analyzing economic issues like State employment problems. Indeed, on theoretical grounds alone, its weaknesses suggest that we should place high priority on developing and considering alternative economic analyses. When we look at the most important structural factors affecting economic change, it may turn out that supply-and-demand adjustments are much *less* important than the economic environment and power which establish the boundaries within which market forces have effect.

Productive Efficiency and Workers' Skills

A second important theoretical perspective informs many traditional discussions of State employment problems. This view pays principal attention to the *characteristics* of workers in different regions, States, and cities, building from analyses of the *supply* of labor in different labor markets. It suggests that firms may have trouble producing efficiently in particular areas if there are too few available workers possessing the skills those firms need. If they can't find the right kinds of workers, they may go out of business or move somewhere else.

During the recent rush of proposals for business tax reduction and investment subsidies, this focus on labor supply and workers' skills has received less attention than in earlier years. During the 1960s, however, economists' preoccupation with workers' skills *dominated* local, State, and federal manpower policy. Almost all public policies designed to solve "employment problems" aimed at improving the skills and working attitudes of less-skilled or "disadvantaged" workers. Although that emphasis no longer dominates public policy in this problem area, the analysis which framed the earlier preoccupation with workers' skills still remains as an important backdrop to current discussions of State employment problems. Several examples illustrate its persistence:

■ Many who discuss employment problems in older central cities ascribe some of the problems of present or potential central city employers to the low skills and poor working habits of ghetto workers. This often leads to the suggestion either that minimum wage levels should be lowered or that firms cannot be attracted to those areas in increasing numbers unless they receive heavy skills-training subsidies.

■ The skills perspective provides a convenient excuse when discussions turn to the millions of workers, particularly those in older central cities, who have difficulty finding work. If their job problems can be attributed to their low skills, then business can comfortably shift the spotlight of employment discussions *to* the workers and *away* from employers. And if one could reasonably argue that individuals are responsible for making basic decisions about how high a skill level they have attained—which economists of the "human capital" school essentially argue—business can even more comfortably allow "blame" for workers' problems to settle onto the workers' shoulders. "What can you expect?", one hears employers asking. "If they didn't have the sense to stay in school and acquire skills, how can they expect to compete in today's job market?"

Those who place special emphasis on the problems of productive efficiency and workers' skills would all agree that there are only two possible solutions to the problems highlighted by this analytic preoccupation: More money should be invested in subsidy of workers' skills improvement; and workers should receive encouragement—mostly called "motivation"—to improve their skills. Since many also argue that skills are best acquired on the job, the former policy suggestion typically devolves into suggestions for subsidies to employers for on-the-job skills training. And both suggestions provide an easy excuse for fatalism: If there is not enough public money

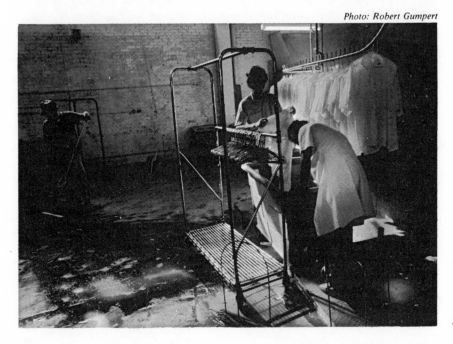

27

available to support skills programs, or if "disadvantaged" workers simply won't commit themselves to their self-improvement, then there is nothing more we can hope to accomplish. You can lead a horse to water, one hears, but you can't make him drink.

There are two main theoretical problems with the workers' skills perspective.

First, the perspective, as typically applied, encourages a critical theoretical mistake in the way it views workers' productivities. A given worker's productivity is actually a function of *two* kinds of factors—the features of the *job* in which the worker is employed and the worker's own *skill* or productivity characteristics. If a brilliant and dextrous college graduate works in a piece-work garment shop, there are obvious limits to his/her productivity. If an "unskilled" worker with little job experience manages to land an auto assembly job, that worker's "productive contribution" to the firm and the economy may suddenly soar—even though the worker has changed neither skills nor attitudes.

In this context, one cannot establish *a priori* whether workers' employment problems should properly be attributed to their own lack of skills and good working attitudes or to the paucity of available jobs which, no matter how low their initial skills, would permit highly productive use of those skills. The way in which traditional analyses typically discuss workers' skills completely overlooks this theoretical indeterminacy. Those analyses suggest, however implicitly, that unemployed or underemployed workers would be able to solve their labor problems on their own if only they learned more and worked harder. In fact, pending more careful investigation, it would be perfectly consistent with this analytic emphasis on workers' productivities to conclude that there is nothing that "disadvantaged" workers could do "on their own" until the supply of "good jobs" dramatically expanded.

The second theoretical problem relates directly to the first. Most traditional analyses of skills dramatically mis-state the kinds of skills which make workers "productive." There are some jobs in the economy, to be sure, which require considerable education, critical intelligence, and problem-solving capacity. (The author's own research suggests that these jobs comprise, at most, one quarter of all jobs in the economy; see below). Most jobs require nothing of the sort. Workers with virtually no skills and no training can easily learn the necessary tasks. What matters most, in those situations, is workers' relative willingness to work hard at relatively undemanding and boring jobs. That willingness depends, in turn, primarily on the job security and monetary rewards available in return. This argument

suggests a quite simple theoretical conclusion. In most jobs, workers' success may have nothing to do with the level of their "cognitive" achievement, or IQ, or reading and writing skills, or manual dexterity, or specific vocational skills, or other attributes conventionally associated with workers' "productivity." Their productivity *and* their success may depend, in contrast, on the wages and job security of the *job* which they find through the labor market. Policies which aim primarily at improving workers' skills, viewed from this consideration, might make little or no difference in improving the job opportunities of more "disadvantaged" workers.

There is also a wide variety of *empirical* evidence one can marshal against the traditional arguments about workers' skills. Three examples of such evidence should help convey the weakness of the traditional concern about "disadvantaged" workers' skills.

First, many studies have found that workers with more education and vocational training earn relatively higher incomes *only* in a narrow range of professional and technical jobs. In at least two-thirds of all occupations in the economy, workers' employment success—measured by their wages or annual incomes—bears almost no relationship to their formal "skills" training and is almost completely determined by the characteristics of the industries and jobs in which they work. Even if their schooling experience has helped channel them into the jobs they have, it is only because firms rely on school degrees **29** as "screening" devices, not because there is anything about their formal skills training which prepares them specifically for the jobs they hold or precludes their learning how to do other kinds of work (Gordon, 1972; and Edwards, 1979).

Second, some pioneering empirical work has documented the critical importance for workers' job success of their *attitudes* to their jobs. One study found that workers' "dependability" and "responsiveness to authority" in middle-level bureaucratic jobs was three times more important in explaining their wages and supervisors' rating than the combined influence of their education, cognitive achievement, or previous formal skills training. Those who were content to accept the behavioral demands of the job did relatively well, while those who weren't were penalized by their employers. "Skill levels" mattered much less (Edwards, 1976).

Doesn't that raise the possibility that there are some workers who have such poor work attitudes that they just can't adjust to the world of work? The third piece of empirical evidence places that question in a very special light. During the late 1960s, many corporations instituted special training programs for "disadvantaged" workers. The results of those experiments were striking and uniform: people with poor work experience blossomed in jobs where they were promised security and advancement, while people with comparable backgrounds grew restive in training and motivational programs which did *not* point directly toward jobs with similar promise (Cohn, 1971). The experience suggested, very concretely, that the horses would drink water if they were convinced that it was the real thing.

These considerations suggest that, for most jobs and workers in the U.S. economy, what matters most is the character of the jobs available. If the job provides decent rewards, workers will be able to perform in them with little additional training and encouragement. If the job provides "indecent" rewards, many if not most workers will prove surprisingly immune to inducements for skills advancement and motivational incentives. If skills and motivation don't matter in some jobs, why should workers care about them anyway?

Mainstream Analysis and the Supply of "Good Jobs"

This initial review of mainstream economic analysis provides enough background to highlight the neoclassical answer to the question motivating this chapter. Although most mainstream economists rarely focus on the question of "good jobs" as such, we can nonetheless infer how they would answer our question, "why aren't there enough good jobs?"[2]

Neoclassical economists would argue, in general, that there is a shortage of "good jobs"—assuming even for a moment that they would accept the arguments of Chapter 1—because of some combination of a *shortage* of skilled workers, suitable technology, or capital funds/profits for investment or higher wages. Each of these possible explanations requires separate attention.

The argument about workers' skills relies on a supply argument. If we define "good jobs" as those which, in particular, pay decent wages and provide adequate job security, then neoclassical economists would argue that employers can only afford to provide "good jobs" if there are workers whose skills and productivity warrant such rewards. It would logically follow, within the neoclassical perspective, that a paucity of "good jobs" must mean—to a very large degree—that there is an insufficient supply of workers with enough skills to justify additional "good jobs."

But there is plenty of evidence which suggests that there has been a growing surplus of workers with very substantial skills and that a corresponding increase in "good jobs" has *not* resulted. Berg (1970) and Freeman (1976) have shown, for example, that the supply of college-educated workers with substantial "general educational" skills has increased steadily since the 1950s, but that the number of jobs utilizing those skills has stagnated. The neoclassical perspective would have suggested that employers should have created jobs which made increasing use of those workers' skills. Nothing of the sort has happened. Similarly, many studies have shown that large numbers of workers in "poor jobs" are very "over-qualified" for those jobs; this surplus supply of relatively skilled labor has not resulted in the creation of more new jobs which would utilize those surplus skills (Gordon, 1972; Edwards, 1979).

There is little convincing evidence, in short, that employers have created more "good jobs" even though there have been increasing supplies of workers with productive skills.

Similar problems confront the second kind of explanation which neoclassical economists would offer for the inadequate supply of "good jobs": that workers' productivity depends not only on their skills but also on the technical support they receive. If workers can work with more machines and coordinate technology, their productivity can increase (even if they have relatively lower skills). If there were more productive technology around, there might be more "good jobs."

The available evidence does not dub this explanation the crown prince of plausibility. Large corporations have been using more and more advanced technology at a continuing rate throughout the post-war period. As we shall see below, however, their use of technology and automation has generally *reduced* the level of employment, not increased it. Moreover, large corporations have increasingly deployed advanced technology in regions and countries where local conditions permit their paying low wages and avoiding union influence. For the time being, at least, it appears that (a) rapid automation tends to eliminate jobs, not to create them; and (b) large corporations are taking advantage of their current leverage over workers to modernize in areas where workers' chances of securing decent wages and adequate leverage over their working conditions are least promising. This suggests that we cannot easily assume that accelerated business investment in new technologies would contribute to the pool of "good jobs" in the United States to any significant degree.

These arguments help frame the third neoclassical argument—that there would be more "good jobs" if businesses had more funds for investment or higher wages. Let us distinguish between small competitive firms and large corporations. Among small businesses, there is no guarantee that an increase in investment funds available to those firms would necessarily create "good jobs"; it may be that the competitive conditions and insecurities confronting those businesses will preclude their creation of "good job" opportunities no matter how rapidly their profits increased. Among large corporations it seems likely, particularly during the current period, that (a) they have adequate capital funds anway (*Fortune* reported that the 500 largest industrial corporations earned profits in 1978 at the highest rate since the mid-1950s); (b) that they are very likely to apply large portions of their available funds to mergers and acquisitions, not to productive investment; and (c) that whatever productive investments they make, for the reasons adduced in the previous paragraphs, are not necessarily likely to generate more "good jobs."

It seems necessary to conclude, in short, that neoclassical economics provides flawed tools for the analysis of employment problems and does not provide a promising explanation for the lack of "good jobs" in the U.S. economy. Isn't there a better way?

A STRUCTURAL ANALYSIS OF EMPLOYMENT PROBLEMS   This section outlines a more promising way of viewing State employment problems. It sketches an alternative structural analysis of the sources of those problems and applies that analysis to the question of the availability of "good jobs."[3] This outline employs three separate building blocks: (1) an analysis of the contours of labor market structure in the U.S. economy; (2) a discussion of the factors influencing regional economic growth and decline; and (3) a brief review of the sources of aggregate economic instability during the 1970s. These three building blocks provide enough material for some relatively clear answers to our questions about the supply of "good jobs"; this synthetic analysis is provided in the fourth part of this section.

Labor Market Structure

A small group of economists (including myself) has recently developed a suggestive analysis of the character and structure of the labor market in the United States.[4] This analysis concludes that there are some major differences among jobs and the labor markets feeding them—among what we call *segments*—which dominate the influence of individual employers' and workers' characteristics. Any analysis of the character of State employment problems, we suggest, must begin from a consideration of the basic structure of the jobs and labor markets within its economy.

What are the segments and where do they come from?

The analysis begins with an appreciation of the fundamental importance of the largest corporations in the economy. The largest 200 industrial corporations control close to two-thirds of all industrial assets. The largest financial and service corporations have nearly comparable power in their respective sectors. These large firms have achieved a size and power in the modern U.S. economy which permits long-term planning and considerable flexibility in how they organize their basic productive operations.* These firms differ significantly from the millions of smaller enterprises which survive on narrower margins; count on much less secure futures; therefore plan over much shorter horizons; and ultimately have much less flexibility in how they structure production and organize the jobs of their workers.

The distinction between these two kinds of firms shows up clearly in basic data on corporate profits. Almost all firms in the U.S. economy earned an average rate of profit during the late 1950s and 1960s of a little more than eight percent per year on capital assets. Firms which were very large *and* which operated in industries dominated by a few firms earned average profit rates of 10.8 percent on capital assets. Firm size, by itself, or industry structure, by itself, didn't matter; profit rates in those cases hovered around the eight percent level. Only if a firm was *both* large *and* shared a "concentrated" industrial structure could it achieve a higher profit level (Edwards, 1979).

---

*I shall refer in all the subsequent discussions to "productive" work and "productive" operations when talking about the basic tasks of producing goods and services—the non-supervisory workers who are counted as "production workers" in government data.

We call those powerful firms "core" firms.

During the period from 1900 through the 1930s, after the first wave of mergers from 1898 to 1902 had created a pool of very large firms, giant corporations tried to use their size and power to control workers in a wide variety of ways—breaking strikes with ethnic workers, using complicated job titles and incentive schemes to pit workers against each other, encouraging craft unions to compete with nascent industrial union movements, relying on arbitrary promotional schemes to push workers into competition for foremen's promotional favors. When the industrial union movement crested and finally broke through employer opposition in the Depression, workers focused much of their protest on some of these "arbitrary" uses and abuses of employers' power. They demanded a rationalization of wage and promotional systems. Once employers began to accept the permanent existence of industrial unions (and World War Two enforced the discipline of war-time cooperation on both the corporations and the unions), a much more structured system of production emerged in many industries as the joint product of large corporate flexibility and large union power. Since those structures seemed to moderate workers' opposition and militance, many other employers—particularly those employing white-collar workers—copied these new systems of rationalized wage and fringe payments, promotion by seniority and experience, and advancement over time. Technological change

Photo: Robert Gumpert

conformed to and helped support the crystallization of these new job structures, permitting wage advancements in structured shops and offices, and eliminating jobs of production workers to save on the costs of these increasingly expensive arrangements. We call the jobs which resulted "primary jobs."

Smaller firms—those which we call "peripheral" (in contrast to "core")—could not match the changes in job structures which large employers were institutionalizing. This led to an increasingly sharp *divergence* between the character of jobs in competitive industries and small firms—like the garment industry, food processing, and wood processing in manufacturing and small offices and retail trade in the service sectors—and those in some parts of core-firm production. The small firms continued traditional systems of production, featuring labor-intensive systems, low wages, little room for advancement, and little margin for union victories. We call these kinds of jobs "secondary" jobs.

Large firms did not organize all sectors of their productive operations along the lines of the new internal structures, however, since they were sometimes able to save money and avoid union influence by retaining secondary organizations. In the tobacco industry, for example, the companies' success in beating the infant industrial union of tobacco workers in 1947-1948 permitted a continuation of the relatively lower wages and insecure job systems which had dominated tobacco work since the late 19th century. Though tobacco firms and steel firms have similar industrial characteristics, workers' job privileges and security in the two industries differ substantially as a result of the differential power of workers in those industries. Steel workers enjoy much higher wages and much better security as a result. And their relative power has helped promote an increasingly structured "internal labor market" since the 1930s.

Core firms operate many "primary" production operations, in short, even though they also retain some secondary operations. Peripheral firms find it extremely difficult to duplicate those systems because of their firm and industry characteristics—even when, as in the case of the garment industry—an industrial union represents their workers. The result is a sharp distinction between the characteristics of *primary* jobs and *secondary* jobs.

One other distinction is important for our analysis. In the 19th and early 20th centuries, workers developed technical skills and general productive knowledge through the *craft* system of apprenticeship. During the early 20th century, when corporations sought to free themselves from their dependence on craft workers, they began to construct alternate paths to technical skill and general competence, **35** building private vocational systems and encouraging technical institutes providing engineering skills. This led directly to the proliferation of general technical training through colleges, universities, and vocational institutes.

By the 1950s, these alternate paths to professional and technical skills were firmly rooted in educational institutions outside of the firm; the site of advanced skills training had shifted, in other words, from internal craft systems to colleges and universities. (Among other advantages to large corporations, the public shared the costs of training workers in colleges and universities through their tax dollars.) Increasingly, professional and technical jobs in large corporations (and other voluntary and public organizations) were located in separate parts of the organization, with different job ladders and ports-of-entry, relying on different kinds of skills and offering different kinds of rewards.

Small firms provide few of these jobs. Large organizations provide most of them. This divergence between jobs requiring more *general* skills and those requiring *routine* skills has led, in our view, to an increasingly sharp distinction among primary jobs between what we call "independent primary" jobs, in which workers have some (relative) autonomy and independence in their work; and "subordinate primary" jobs in which workers execute routine tasks strictly according to rule and the commands of their supervisors.

With these distinctions, it is possible to summarize our analysis of the main kinds of work in the U.S. economy. Below are listed these segments along with a brief characterization of the kinds of jobs within them and the labor markets feeding them.

■ *Independent primary* jobs: Technical, professional, managerial, and craft jobs; requiring some general skills and problem-solving abilities; high pay with some job security; rewards to personal characteristics of initiative and general analytic ability. Technical and professional jobs fed by labor markets beginning with the formal education screening process and then reproduced through screening process based both on credentials and work experience. Craft jobs still fed through apprenticeship systems.

■ *Subordinate primary* jobs: Decent pay and substantial job security; low general skill requirements; some skills learned on the job through experience; authority relations and internal job structures very important fulcrum for corporate administration of production process and individuals' personal advancement. Workers get such jobs through personal contacts as much as through formal labor market processes, and advancement comes much more easily through internal promotion than job-shopping in the external labor market.

■ *Secondary* jobs: In small firms or small shops/offices of large firms; low pay; few skills required; no opportunity for advancement; virtually no inducements for workers to remain on the job. Jobs filled through casual and virtually random general labor market shape-ups and advertisement. (Employment offices also feed workers into these jobs.)

What are the relative sizes of these three segments? Using data from the 1970 Census to estimate their relative size, we reach several conclusions. Of all those counted as "economically active" in the 1970 Census, 92 percent were employed and 8 percent were self-employed. Table 1 provides a complete distribution of the 92 percent who were employed among the three main segments identified by the analysis of labor market structure discussed in the preceding paragraphs:

Table 1
The Distribution of Employment, 1970

	Number of Employed Workers (in millions)	Percent of Total Employment
Independent Primary Jobs	22.466	32.5%
Subordinate Primary Jobs	21.144	30.6
Secondary Jobs	25.541	36.9
	69.151	100.0%

SOURCE: Data from *1970 Census of Population.* Definitions and compilation from Gordon (1980a).

What is striking about these figures, at first glance, is the large size of each of the three segments—none is an insignificant or insubstantial fraction of the total labor force—and the continuing size and relative importance of the secondary segment—the largest of the three and accounting for more than a third of the entire labor force.

The full implications of this analysis will be summarized in a following section. For now, four main conclusions seem most important.

First, both blue-collar and white-collar jobs are important in all three segments. Both garment work and the typing pool exemplify secondary work. Both steel work and book-keeping jobs typify subordinate primary jobs. Both electricians and doctors illustrate the **37** independent primary segment. In the data for the 1970 census, all three segments are divided between blue-collar and white-collar jobs in roughly comparable proportions. Table 2 provides these distributions:

Table 2
The Distribution of Factory and Office Employment, 1970[a]

	Blue-Collar Employment		White-Collar Employment	
	Number (in millions)	Percent of Total	Number (in millions)	Percent of Total
Independent Primary Jobs	7.094	29.0%	15.370	35.1%
Subordinate Primary Jobs	6.820	27.8	14.324	32.8
Secondary Jobs	10.584	43.1	14.042	32.1
	24.498	100.0%	43.736	100.0%

a) The total figures exclude those tabulated as agricultural employees and unpaid household employees.

SOURCE: Data from *1970 Census of Population*. Definitions and compilations from Gordon (1980a).

Second, the analysis of segmentation helps clarify some of the important differences between private and public employment. Public jobs are also distributed among the three segments. The difference in the distribution, however, is that more public jobs are independent primary jobs—obviously reflecting the large concentration of teaching and health professionals and technicians in the public sector—and that correspondingly fewer are secondary workers—also partly reflecting community and union pressure for minimally decent pay in lower-level public jobs. See Table 3 for these distributions.

Third, the principal determinants of the existence of these differences among segments lie in the characteristics of *firms* and the *job systems* they employ, not in the characteristics of different workers. Workers in the subordinate primary and secondary segments differ remarkably little in terms of skills, for example; those in the former segment have simply been lucky enough to land jobs providing higher wages and more structured advancement opportunities (Gordon, 1980a).

Fourth, the structures defining jobs within each of the segments are *not* very flexible, *not* easily adjusted to changing labor market conditions or labor supply proportions. The historical processes through which these divergent conditions emerged have meant that **38** firms cannot easily change the ways in which they organize production

Table 3
The Distribution of Public and Private Employment, 1970

	Private-Sector Employment		Public-Sector Employment	
	Number (in millions)	Percent of Total	Number (in millions)	Percent of Total
Independent Primary Jobs	17.885	30.8%	4.581	41.3%
Subordinate Primary Jobs	17.372	29.9	3.772	34.0
Secondary Jobs	22.801	39.3	2.740	24.7
	58.058	100.0%	11.093	100.0%

SOURCE: Data from *1970 Census of Population.* Definitions and compilations from Gordon (1980a).

or hire and promote workers.

Two examples illustrate this general point:

■ One study of welders in a shipbuilding yard found that the firm could have saved money on welders by hiring skilled welders from outside the firm rather than training them through internal apprenticeship systems. The firm would have needed to pay higher wages to welders than it was currently paying, however, because of the higher external wage. The rigidity of its internal wage structure meant that those higher wages to welders would have to be translated into higher wages for every other production worker. The savings on welder training costs they might have realized could not be generalized because of the interdependence between welders' wages and all other wages within the firm (Ryan, 1977).

■ In the computer business, the distinction between the independent primary segment and the subordinate primary segment is illustrated by the difference in job tasks and skill requirements between "systems analysts" and "processing programmers." Over the past 15 years, computer firms have encountered substantial problems whenever they sought to downgrade the tasks of individual systems analysts' jobs because systems analysts have clear and unyieldingly high expectations about the quality of their work. As a result, they have often been forced to restructure the operations of an entire shop completely, changing the organization of work tasks from top to bottom, in order to save money on systems analysts' jobs; their employees' expectations limited their freedom to make small changes and forced them to make major ones. Once the distinction between systems analysis and *39* programming took root in the 1950s and early 1960s, firms were caught in a web of their own creation (Kraft, 1977; Greenbaum, 1979).

Regional Investment and Disinvestment

The preceding analysis has clear implications for the analysis of forces affecting the supply of different kinds of jobs—both "good jobs" and "poor jobs"; these implications will be elaborated in the final section of this chapter. But State policymakers must be concerned not only with the structure of available employment but also with its location. What forces account for the geographic distribution of "good jobs"? In particular, what can we learn about the sources of the recently accelerating shift of employment to the Sunbelt?[5]

Many media accounts treat the flow of jobs to the Sunbelt as a recent phenomenon, beginning in the late 1960s. In fact, the rise of the Sunbelt began during and immediately after World War Two. Studies of manufacturing location during the 1950s and 1960s all noted the most important difference between pre-War and post-War patterns: there had been a sudden shift to the South and Southwest during the 1940s.

What accounted for this shift? One could hardly attribute it to the energy crisis of 1974. There had not yet been a flood of older people to the sunshine. What had changed?

Photo: Earl Dotter/ALEC

I have argued elsewhere that critical changes in the geographic pattern of firm location have flowed historically from corporate efforts to find new ways of gaining more control over their employees and escaping from mounting worker unrest (Gordon, 1978, and 1980b).

One significant moment in this history came at the very end of the 19th century. Firms had been locating in the downtown factory districts of the largest industrial cities like New York, Philadelphia, Chicago, and other new Midwestern cities. During the 1880s and 1890s, workers' protests grew rapidly, spilling into the streets of the central city factory districts. The factories and workers' housing districts were so densely packed that "strike fevers" seemed to spread like contagious diseases. Increasingly, employers began to long for an escape from the central cities in order to avoid these disruptions.

The merger movement of 1898-1902 created firms of sufficient scale and assets to afford such moves. What were then called "industrial satellite suburbs" (such as Gary, Indiana) began springing up on the outskirts of the largest manufacturing cities. For the first time in the history of the United States, manufacturing employment began growing more rapidly in the "rings" of large cities than in the "centers." The decentralization of manufacturing had begun.

One cannot attribute this early dispersal of factories to the early development of the truck, since all transportation economists agree that the truck was not a viable freight substitute for the railroad until the 1920s. Nor can one attribute it to new land-intensive technologies like the assembly line which placed a new premium on less expensive land in the suburbs; there is no evidence that the technologies used in the suburbs were more land-intensive, and there is even some evidence suggesting that the opposite tendency prevailed.

My own argument turns conventional interpretations on their head, and suggests a substantially different view of manufacturing decentralization. Rather than accepting the traditional notion that the truck and new technologies encouraged and permitted the movement of factories out of the central cities, I would argue that employers' initial flight from labor unrest called forth the development of the truck and eventually permitted the development of more land-intensive technologies.

Once the movement to the satellite suburbs began, of course, the general pattern of urban investment and disinvestment began to structure the satellite suburbs into the system. Suburban plants were more modern and often more efficient simply because they were newer. Employment continued to grow rapidly on the outskirts of the largest cities. Central business districts became more and more **41** specialized in office and service functions. Coupled with the end to suburban annexation at the turn of the century, the manufacturing decentralization helped create increasing political fragmentation, with metropolitan areas becoming patchwork quilts of overlapping political jurisdictions. The titles of two noted books about this era in metropolitan development, Robert Woods' *1400 Governments* (1959) and Robert Fogelson's *The Fragmented Metropolis* (1967), evoke this pattern of increasing fragmentation.

The industrial union movement of the 1930s threw a monkey-wrench into that pattern. The unions were forced to develop industrial strategies to overcome the isolation of workers in industrial plants and the divisions which fragmented patterns of industrial locations created. Once the CIO unions succeeded in linking up and uniting these dispersed groups of workers, employers lost a critical advantage they had held and exploited for nearly 40 years. Growing evidence suggests that they made another critical decision—wherever and however possible, they would begin creating the possibility for movement away from the regions where workers had achieved the greatest strength.

World War Two proved to be a turning point. During the War, the federal government helped subsidize billions of dollars of new plant construction and infrastructural development. Much of it was located in the South and Southwest, certainly a far higher proportion than the previous proportions of total industrial capital investment in those areas. After the War, the federal government turned much of that plant and equipment over to private corporations. A sudden and significant shift in the geographic distribution of industrial capital had been achieved. Particularly after the passage of the Taft-Hartley Act in 1947, with its proscription of secondary boycotts and sanction for State right-to-work laws, large corporations had a new leg up on the industrial unions. Increasingly during the post-War years, they were able to plan plants and output expansion with a careful eye to the relative militance of Northern (unionized) workers and the relative quiescence of Southern (non-unionized) workers.

Once again, these initial geographic shifts were frozen into infrastructural steel and concrete. Sunbelt capital and infrastructure, since it was newer, was in many cases more efficient. Disproportionate infrastructural investment was flowing to the Sunbelt. The older capital of the Northwest was not being maintained, both in the central cities and in the suburban factory belts established after the turn of the century.

The impact of this differential pattern of regional investment and disinvestment was not immediately noticed, of course, because continuing post-War prosperity permitted the continued utilization of capital structures and equipment of both *more* and *less* recent vintage. It was only during the late 1960s, when corporate profit margins began to narrow and foreign competition became more threatening, that firms began to shift plant utilization more rapidly. The acceleration of the movement of manufacturing employment to the Sunbelt coincided with the growing uncertainty in the economy around 1968-69. But that accelerated movement would itself have been nearly impossible if it had not built upon and taken advantage of the longer-term construction of an industrial base and infrastructure in the Sunbelt states.

As with the earlier discussion of labor market segmentation, this discussion of regional investment and disinvestment will be more fully applied to a discussion of current State employment problems in a subsequent section. Two important points seem most important as background for that later synthesis.

First, this account places critical emphasis on the importance of private and public *infrastructural* investment as the *foundation* for the growth of manufacturing within and among geographic regions. Significant shifts in the geographic location of manufacturing activity cannot take place without significant changes in the historic pattern of industrial investment and infrastructural facilities. Those decisions do not come through gradual evolution and accretion; rather, they reflect qualitative and purposeful decisions by powerful decision-makers with access to the capital assets necessary to launch new patterns of investment. Neither the decentralization of manufacturing at the turn of the century nor the first construction of Sunbelt capital during and after World War Two occurred by accident or as the product of inadvertent "exogenous" shifts in people's preferences. Nor were these shifts induced by the marginal enticements of State and local tax subsidies and incentives. Rather, these historic shifts in the pattern of capital investment reflected decisive steps by private and public decision-makers to mobilize capital resources in new directions. If one wanted to have some opposite effect on the geographic distribution of economic resources, one would have to mobilize private and public decisions affecting capital resources on a comparable scale.

Second, this account suggests that such shifts are not likely to reflect historically and politically "neutral" decisions, guaranteed to benefit all citizens in equal proportions. I have argued that corporate efforts to flee from workers' growing power have played a critical role in channeling new patterns of capital investment.

In order to make room for a novel and potentially controversial argument, I have undoubtedly simplified the complex of historic **43** forces which paved the way to new patterns of capital investment. But it remains clear, in my view, that corporate efforts to achieve new leverage in their continuing battles with their employees played a decisive role. As far as their workers were concerned—not to mention the workers' families and surrounding communities—the corporate decision to change venue was hardly benevolent. Those corporate policies arose from corporate decisions to take advantage of their access to capital funds in order to improve their bargaining power with their workers (and their unions). The decline of relative union power during the late 1950s and 1960s, as well as the difficult bargaining position in which industrial unions now find themselves, bears partial witness to the importance of these historic developments.

More Than Just An Impending Recession

A third piece of analysis is necessary to complete the background for an alternative account of the sources of current State employment problems. This piece of analysis builds from a concern with the character of the economic instability which presently plagues the U.S. (and world) economy.[6]

Many conventional economists and public officials continue to talk as if the current dynamic of recession and recovery is "more of the same," susceptible to the same kinds of macro-economic instruments as the business cycles of the 1950s and 1960s. But evidence belies that complacence. There are mounting signs that the kind of macro-economic dynamic currently driving the economies of the advanced countries differs sharply from the pattern of stable growth and continued prosperity in the first two post-War decades.

One piece of evidence is obvious. The "trade-off" between inflation and unemployment has experienced virtually complete transformation. We used to get less inflation with greater unemployment, and vice versa. Now we get more inflation and more unemployment than we have had for years, without anything like the obvious inverse relationship which characterized them during the 1950s and 1960s.

Other indications draw more attention in the business press than in the public media.

First, business investment in real "structures and equipment" has been stagnating since 1976. One can compare the rate of real business investment since the trough of the recession in 1974-75 with investment at comparable points in recoveries during other business cycles in the post-War years. As both *Business Week* and *Fortune* have observed several times in special issues, that comparison shows that the business sector is investing at a far *slower* rate than during any other post-War "recovery." Corporate profits are high and their capital funds are very

Photo: Earl Dotter/ALEC

liquid, but they're buying up companies and engaging in commodities and currency speculation rather than building factories and machines.

Second, most business analysts agree that corporate investment is lagging at least partly because of corporate fears about the political and economic climate in their traditional turfs. As a result of threats to their continued privileges, corporations have been moving their capital overseas at an accelerating rate. The symptom is contraction in traditional industrial locations. The evidence lies in the accelerating expansion to the Sunbelt and the extraordinary increases in U.S. corporate overseas investment since the mid-1960s.

Third, the stagnation of investment and the rapid redistribution of investment have contributed to a growing unpredictability and instability in world trade. Traditional trading patterns have been unsettled. The world market seems more and more like a kaleidoscope.

Fourth, this has contributed to precarious monetary instability in the world economy. The value of the dollar has plummeted. Other currencies are fluctuating rapidly. Eurodollar market speculation remains unchecked. Third World debt to the World Bank and other banks remains a critical problem and a potential source of international instability. Most international financial authorities admit that there are no easy answers to these sources of uncertainty.

All of these signs, taken together, suggest an economy which is not behaving "normally" at all and which cannot easily "recover" from these destabilizing dynamics. They point to some increasingly evident signs that the economy's private mechanisms for investment and production are not working as they did during the 1950s and 1960s, that some kind of collective private and public action will be necessary to reverse a dynamic of growing instability.

This should not be surprising if we view the world economy from a historical perspective. There have been successive stages of alternating prosperity and stagnation since the 18th century. It appears that one of the main sources of those alternating cycles has been the effect of concentrated infrastructural and commercial investment after a period of stagnation and before a period of sustained prosperity. Around the turn of the century and again after World War Two, heavy and concentrated investment in the infrastructure—particularly in transportation and communication networks—helped fuel the new waves of prosperity and rapid investment during the succeeding decades. Inevitably, the extra fuel provided by those investment episodes burned itself out and the economy was caught in another ebb of stagnation and increasing economic uncertainty.

The lesson of those earlier episodes seems fairly clear. A new level of collective organization has been necessary on each occasion to wrest the economy from the dynamic of spreading stagnation. At the turn of the century, corporate mergers and the intervention of the New York banks provided that impetus. During and after World War Two, federal discipline and capital funding helped rescue the economy from the slough of the Depression. If these historic parallels have any meaning for the current period, they suggest that some kind of active and guided intervention will prove necessary to help guide the economy back onto a stable track.

The question raised by those lessons, of course, is *whose intervention in whose interests?* Multinational corporations have been acting in their own interests and have apparently concluded that their own interests are best served by a rapid movement of capital to other countries. It is not at all clear that public policies to deal with State employment problems can rely on multinational corporations—or the largest domestic corporations—to move in directions which will serve any other interests beyond their own. This suggests that State governments cannot easily assume that subsidies and support for private business in their own backyards will either have the kinds of effects they have had in the 1950s and 1960s or exert sufficient influence, on their own, to alter the trajectory of corporate responses to a continuing international economic crisis.

Why Aren't There Enough "Good Jobs" —A Structural Interpretation

Our structural analysis of employment problems has been developed in three stages.

■ The first section argued that the segmentation of jobs has created important inflexibilities in the U.S. labor market. Many jobs do not reward individual workers' initiative or skills and cannot easily be changed. Other jobs—what we call primary jobs—provide opportunities for decent incomes and advancement. Because of the rigidities of job structures in primary segments, however, the basic supply of those jobs, not the skills or attitudes of workers in them, determine their availability. Changes in the basic supply of primary jobs, not changes in the supply characteristics of workers, would be necessary to increase the number of "good jobs."

■ The second section reviewed the history and dynamics of urban and regional growth in the United States. The analysis suggested that structural forces have more influence on regional economic fortunes than quantitative variations in factors like taxes and energy costs. Major shifts in firm location have followed from corporate efforts to evade workers' control. Those evasions have triggered dramatic   **47** changes in the flow of capital for modernization and infrastructural investment. Those capital shifts, in turn, have generated changes in the relative "efficiency" of firms in differing regions. One could not influence the relative efficiency of firms in different regions, according to this argument, without first affecting the character of infrastructural capital investments among regions.

■ The third section suggested that the current crisis of growth and investment is itself a structural crisis—whose resolution will eventually require the kinds of massive and coordinated interventions which finally fostered recovery from the Depression of the 1930s. Special breaks, subsidies, and incentives provided to business on an uncoordinated basis will not be enough to stimulate greater economic activity. Instead, direct and coordinated intervention on a substantial scale will probably be required to affect the current climate of economic instability and to provide sufficient encouragement for further investment and growth.

These arguments can be combined, finally, to provide a structural answer to our recurrent question about the supply of "good jobs." The answer in its simplest form is straightforward: *The economy does not provide an adequate supply of "good jobs" because the structure of the modern economy, and particularly its domination by several hundred giant corporations, neither promotes nor permits the generation of "good jobs."*

This simple conclusion can be developed through several separate steps of elaboration.

The Definition of Good Jobs. In Chapter 1, we defined a "good job" as one which provides adequate wages and fringe benefits; job security and stable employment; decent working conditions; and opportunities for both advancement and control. Most influential discussions of "good jobs," like Ginsberg's 1977 article, collapse this definition into a one-dimensional wage criterion, but we have learned that a complex of factors affect the quality of employment; wages are only one reflection of job quality.

Our analysis above suggests that a working definition of "good jobs" should be based on the structural characteristics which permit individual success and advancement. It would seem to make sense, therefore, to define "good jobs" as *primary* jobs and "poor jobs" as *secondary* jobs precisely in order to emphasize the roots of job quality in the economic structures which influence the organization of production.

Are our observations on the separate dimensions of employment problems from Chapter 1 consistent with this equation of "good jobs" with primary jobs and "poor jobs" with secondary jobs?

■ Decent employment income would require, according to most economists, a regular wage which on a full-time basis provides enough for a household to support itself at levels above or equal to the BLS "lower-than-moderate" budget standard. Roughly one-third of U.S. workers are employed in jobs paying less than this wage level (Gordon, 1977). This seems to fit with the estimate in this chapter that roughly one-third of U.S. employees in 1970 held secondary jobs.

■ Employment security essentially requires that workers be able to work full-time, year-round if they choose. Only two-thirds of U.S. employees work full-time, year-round. While more than ten million workers have part-time jobs because they prefer part-time work, there are probably an equivalent number of secondary workers—particularly older ones—who work full-time at their jobs simply because they have learned that job shopping is unlikely to improve their work prospects (Gordon, 1980a; Edwards, 1979). Thus, our association of "poor jobs" which expose workers to actual or potential employment insecurity with secondary jobs also seems consistent with the aggregate data.

■ Indecent working conditions are more difficult to measure because data are not easily available on the "health-and-safety characteristics" of different jobs. A recent study by Luft (1978) found a substantial correlation between those who suffer occupational disease or injury and those who experience poverty for substantial periods of time.

Photo: Dorothea Lange

These are apparently workers whose fringe benefits or access to insurance is sufficiently limited that they get trapped in the vicious circle of low incomes and poor health. Luft's data seem roughly consistent with the notion that those in secondary jobs bear the greatest risk of real loss of earning capacity from indecent working conditions.

■ Only one-quarter of the U.S. labor force belongs to unions. This obviously does not mean that three-quarters of the labor force work at "poor jobs" providing little job control. Indeed, many large employers have improved working conditions precisely to prevent the spread of unionization. What seems apparent, from the available literature on segmentation, is that (a) *independent primary* workers attain some control over their working conditions because of the importance of their positions and their particular skills—whether or not they belong to unions; (b) that blue-collar workers in the *subordinate primary* segment have been able to take advantage of the room for union influence which the structure of their jobs permits, while white-collar workers (at least in the private sector) have not yet followed that path; while (c) even unionized workers in the secondary sector, like garment workers, are rarely able to translate their union power into full job control or decent working conditions. (See Kerr, 1979, for a detailed analysis of union impact in the primary and secondary segments.) It seems appropriate to conclude that the structure of job segments is at least as important as unionization by itself in establishing the framework within which workers may or may not acquire significant influence over their working and living conditions.

In short, it seems feasible to treat "primary jobs" as "good jobs." In 1970, as we saw above, 63.1 percent of wage-and-salary employees worked in "good jobs." The remaining 36.9 percent of wage-and-salary employees worked in secondary jobs, or what we can call "poor jobs."*

The Barriers to Good Jobs. This definition clearly indicates that we need to pursue the issue of the supply of "good jobs" in two steps: Why can't secondary employers provide "good jobs" instead of "poor" ones? And why don't primary employers provide more "good jobs" than they do?

The segmentation literature provides fairly clear answers to the first

---

*The techniques used to categorize workers are somewhat complicated. Gordon (1980a) presents a full description of the method. It essentially relies on an industry-by-occupation analysis of job characteristics, separating between core and peripheral industries on the one hand and between jobs providing room for the application of workers' skills (or on-the-job skill acquisition) and those neither rewarding nor offering skills development on the other. In both cases, the method of categorization relies on the characteristics of jobs—of industries and occupations—and not on the characteristics, like race, sex, age, or schooling, of workers who hold those jobs.

question. Many secondary employers are small firms in competitive industries. Their small assets make it difficult for them to finance or afford the kinds of improvements in machinery and job structures which would permit higher wages, greater job security, and better working conditions. Perhaps more important, the continuing competition to which they are exposed tends to keep profit margins very low—holding firms very close to the edge of survival. Their thin profit margins make higher wages and greater employment security problematic, much less the kinds of changes in machinery and job structures which would reproduce primary working conditions over the longer term.[7]

In other words, most secondary employers cannot provide good jobs because their firm and industry structure precludes it. Small firms still exhibit the kinds of working conditions which were nearly universal in the late 19th and early 20th centuries. "Good jobs" are better today because large firms and large unions have combined to create a new kind of firm and job structure which permit "good jobs." Small firms in competitive industries are essentially barred from that kind of qualitative transformation.

The second question requires a somewhat more extended answer. Three points seem essential.

First, many large firms find it uneconomical to provide more "good jobs" because it costs more to hire new workers than to extend the hours of current employees. Their fixed costs of providing decent wages and working conditions—embodied in fringe benefits, taxes, and insurance payments—have shifted the calculus of employment toward hiring current employees for longer hours rather than hiring new employees for shorter hours. This explains why many manufacturing firms make such heavy use of overtime, and why average hours worked per week in manufacturing have remained constant during the post World War Two period while average hours per week in some other industries, such as retail trade, have continued to fall.

Second, many large firms actually operate many secondary operations when and where they can. Large clerical employers maintain "poor jobs" in their typing pools and office maintenance operations. Some large manufacturing firms, like electrical, tobacco, and some textile manufacturers, offer essentially secondary employment because they have been able to tap groups of workers whose personal characteristics—foreign workers or women—or their geographic location—Southern workers or isolated undocumented workers in large ghettos—have undercut those workers' ability to translate firm and industry characteristics into "good jobs." If and **51**

Photo: United Auto Workers

when the unionizing drive against J.P. Stevens succeeds, it will be interesting to observe what kinds of changes in job structure occur and how rapidly those changes take place.

There is a third point which is at once more important and more difficult to state persuasively. Essentially, large employers don't want to provide many good jobs *even when they can*. Large employers have invested billions of dollars since the turn of the century in machines and management techniques which improve their control over their workers (Braverman, 1974; Edwards, 1979). Workers have responded by seeking better working conditions and more reliable and predictable systems of hiring, promotion, and work supervision. To the degree that large firms have been forced to accept this increased worker influence, they have moved to reduce their dependence on such "powerful" workers. Large corporations have continually undercut

52 professional workers' status and control, for example, whenever they could afford such changes (Kraft, 1977; Greenbaum, 1979). And large manufacturers continually substitute machines for workers when the technology and investment funds are available. Wherever possible, in short, large firms tend to limit the number of "primary workers" they hire for any given level of labor demand (through more overtime and fewer new hires), and they tend to reduce their aggregate demand for labor through automation and job reorganization when those steps are consistent with other firm objectives. Large corporations are interested in both efficiency *and* control, in other words, and large firms are likely to display a consistent preference, given the choice, for employing fewer (relatively) powerful workers.

The structural argument emerges: The character of competition and the vulnerability of small firms makes it virtually impossible for many secondary employers to "up-grade" the quality of the jobs they provide. And while large firms at least have the potential for providing "good jobs," the logic and requirements of control in large corporations lead them to minimize the number of "good jobs" they provide at any given level of output and investment. The structure of competition and the power of large corporations, in these respects, place stringent limits on the supply of "good jobs."

Evidence for the Structural Argument. Because this structural argument has emerged relatively recently, few studies have yet marshaled or analyzed the kinds of data which would be necessary to test these structural hypotheses fully. There are some fragmentary pieces of evidence, nonetheless, which provide strong preliminary support for this explanation of the paucity of "good jobs."

It is fairly clear, first of all, that the problem stems from the basic structure of the economy and not from the recent years of stagnation and instability. We can look at the period of rapid economic growth between 1948 and 1968, before "stagflation" emerged. During those years, the adult civilian population (and therefore the potential labor force) grew by 30 million. If we eliminate the growth in total employment which was due either to direct government employment or to the employment-generating effects of government expenditures, it turns out that private-sector-generated employment grew by only 2 million over those 20 years. Even when the economy is growing rapidly, in other words, the tendency for many firms to *reduce* employment nearly outweighs the additional employment created by continuing growth.

Moreover, no matter how we measure the distinction between "good" and "poor jobs," it appears that most of the new jobs created by the private economy over the past decades have been "poor jobs," not "good ones." Ginzberg (1977) reaches striking conclusions by applying his earnings criterion to employment changes between 1950 and 1976. He estimates that private sector employment expanded by 25.3 million between 1950 and 1976 (he does not subtract employment generated by government expenditures). Of those new jobs he estimates that 18.2 million were "poor jobs" and only 7.1 were "good jobs"—a ratio of more than 2.5 "poor jobs" for every one "good job." In contrast, he estimates that of the 9 million increase in government employment, there were two new "good jobs" for every one new "poor job." Of the total increase in employment of 34.3 million over those 26 years, only 7.1 were "good jobs" provided by the private sector—a ratio of barely more than one in five. Based on these data, Ginzberg concludes that "we cannot assume that the private sector will be able to create adequate numbers of new jobs." His conclusions about the likelihood of the private sector's generating adequate numbers of new *"good jobs"* flow even more emphatically.

Neither of these first pieces of evidence draws directly on data about firms. This is a substantial disadvantage, since much of the structural argument hinges on differences among firms and not among industries.

Employment analysts have recently paid considerable attention to a new source of data about firm employment patterns developed and analyzed by David Birch and associates at MIT (1979). Many have taken great solace from the Birch data, because they seem superficially to indicate that the private sector still generates millions of jobs through vibrant and dynamic entrepreneurial initiative. Birch's emphasis on the "vitality and job generating powers" of small and independent firms seems to provide substantial encouragement for advocates of free enterprise and the power of competition.

These superficial readings of the Birch data are misplaced. A closer reading suggests, as Birch himself comes close to admitting, that these detailed data on more than five million firms provide relatively striking confirmation of the structural argument outlined in the preceding pages. All of the following facts come from Birch (1979).

■ There is an enormous amount of gross employment change in the U.S. economy. Each year, there is a net loss of roughly eight percent of total employment as a result of firm "deaths" or employment contractions. This means that we must pay careful attention not only to the forces which create jobs but also to the sources of continuing job loss.

■ A very high proportion of net job creation in the economy is generated by small "independent" firms—firms with 20 or fewer employees which are not owned by larger firms. Over the entire period analyzed between 1969 and 1976, there were 6.8 million net jobs created in the private sector. Of those jobs, 67 percent were generated by firms with 20 or fewer employees and 52 percent by "independent" firms with 20 or fewer employees. By contrast, firms with more than 100 employees accounted for only 18.5 percent of net employment change—even though they account for half of total employment. The table below compares these figures with the distribution of total employment in 1973 (based on Social Security data).

Table 4
Total Employment and Employment Growth

Firm Size[a]	Percent of Total Employment 1973	Percent of Net Employment Growth 1969-1976
0-20	24.3%	66.0%
21-100	25.9	15.5
101-500	24.3	5.2
500 plus	25.5	13.3
	100.0%	100.0%

a) The size categories for the distribution of *total* employment are actually 0-19; 20-99; 100-499; and 500+.

SOURCE: Total Employment—*Nation's Business,* 1978, p. 50; employment growth—Birch, 1979; p. 30.

■ Although small firms generate a large percentage of employment, they do not provide "good jobs." Other data show clearly that small establishments provide a disproportionate number of *secondary* jobs; on this basis, we can presumably assume that most small firms' jobs are "poor jobs."[8] Birch's data make clear, moreover, that the jobs generated by small independent firms also provide very unreliable employment since the firms themselves are extremely vulnerable to bankruptcy or layoffs:

■ Of all firms with 20 or fewer employees, 57.8 percent "died" during the seven years studied. Even though small firms grow, they also collapse with alarming frequency. Those who garner jobs with small firms enter at their own risk.

■ Even those small firms which manage to survive an initial period of incubation are no longer very likely to provide employment growth. Of those firms with 20 or fewer employees which had **55** already survived for more than four years at the beginning of the period, only one-third produced net employment growth over the seven-year period.

■ Of all 1.2 million firms in the sample with 20 or fewer employees, only 82,396, or seven percent, sustained "large" employment growth over the growth years from 1969 through 1974. Many firms had some growth for shorter periods, but virtually none were able to generate sizable gains on a continuing basis.

■ In short, the firms which account for employment growth are very unlikely to provide a steady supply of stable jobs over time—regardless of the wages, working conditions, or job control provided in those jobs—simply because the economic condition of those firms is so precarious. To quote Birch's own conclusion:

> The dynamic, growing firm is the one that is frequently taking gambles, that is as likely as not to suffer severe downturns, and that is tough or wise enough to survive them. Having grown, it is just as likely to decline again in the future. In short, it is a banker's nightmare. [Even the stable firm that] minds its business and repays its loans in fact is offering a false sense of security, and is more likely than not to go out of business leaving the bank holding the bag.

■ While large firms are much more stable—only 23 percent of firms with more than 500 employees 'died" between 1969 and 1976—they do

Photo: Robert Gumpert

not generate many jobs. Of firms with more than 500 employees and at least ten years' experience, only 35 percent showed a net increase in employment during the period, while 65 percent either died or contracted their total employment. Firms with more than 500 employees and either branches or subsidiaries—which obviously includes all of the 500 largest corporations in the U.S.—accounted for only ten percent of all net employment increase over the study period.

■ Perhaps more important, large corporations have been rapidly shifting their operations to areas where workers have much more difficulty sustaining influence over their jobs. (As Birch makes clear, these movements are not actual "migrations"—what workers would call "runaways"—but the relative expansion and contraction of branches and subsidiaries.) This effect can be demonstrated with a "shift-share" analysis of Birch's data. (Based on Appendix Table C in Birch, 1979.)

From 1969 to 1976, total employment grew in the Northeast region by only 411,000, in the North Central region by 1.674 million, and in the South and West combined by 4.673 million. What explains the disproportionate share of the Sunbelt in total employment growth? As Birch notes, services grew throughout the nation (and helped save the Northeast). The critical shift in employment took place in manufacturing, where the Northeast and North Central regions lost 710,000 total jobs in just seven years and the Sunbelt gained 335,000. Other job shifts followed from these.

If this was due to a more favorable climate in the Sunbelt for the small independent firms which accounted for so much employment growth, then we would expect that there would be a net "shift" to the Sunbelt of employment growth in small manufacturing firms—with those small independent firms generating many more jobs than one would expect if all regions shared equally in total national employment growth. It turns out, however, that this shift in small firms' growth rates had a relatively small effect. Small independent manufacturing employment grew at moderate rates throughout all four main regions. Over the full seven years, there was a net shift to the Sunbelt of only 88,000 manufacturing jobs in small independent firms.

In contrast, the Northeast and North Central regions suffered much larger shifts of large firm manufacturing away to the Sunbelt. If the Frostbelt regions had suffered merely their expected losses of manufacturing employment over the period, they would have lost 232,000 manufacturing jobs in firms with more than 100 employees with branches of subsidiaries. Instead, they lost a total of 710,000 jobs provided by large multiplant firms. This means that large firms (with more than 100 employees and branches or subsidiaries) *shifted* 478,000   **57** manufacturing jobs to the Sunbelt in just seven years—more than five times the shift attributable to the differential fortunes of small independent firms. As Birch also notes, this differential expansion does not reflect a shift of headquarters to the Sunbelt. In the South, for example, 72 percent of branch employment growth was controlled by firms headquartered in the Northeast or North Central region. Large multiplant firms chose, in other words, to shift their manufacturing investment to areas where they felt more comfortable.

Despite all this specific detail, the main contours of our analysis emerge fairly clearly. Small firms generate many jobs but few of those jobs are either "good jobs" or reliable sources of employment. Large firms provide relatively few jobs and, in addition, have been rapidly reallocating their resources to areas where workers have much more trouble ensuring decent working conditions. Birch's own conclusions confirm our analysis:

> It is no wonder that efforts to stem the tide of job decline have been so frustrating and largely unsuccessful. [On the one hand] the very spirit that gives [small firms] their vitality and job-generating powers is the same spirit that makes them unpromising partners for the development administrator. [On the other hand] the easier strategy of working with larger, 'known' corporations whose behavior is better understood will not be, and has not been, very productive. Few of the net new jobs generated in our economy are generated by this group. Furthermore, the larger corporations, using their financial strength, are the first to redistribute their operations out of declining areas into growing ones... There is no clear way out of this quandary.

Many State policymakers may be reluctant to accept these conclusions, but they flow naturally from our analysis. The private sector *cannot* generate an adequate supply of good jobs for two critical reasons: 1) Those firms who *could* provide "good jobs" do not generate much net employment over time and prefer to reduce their relative reliance on workers holding "good jobs." 2) Those firms which tend to provide net increases in employment in the economy are either too small or too unstable to provide "good jobs." As long as large corporations maintain the kind of economic control over basic investment which they currently possess, and as long as intense competition assaults smaller enterprises, the scarcity of "good jobs" seems destined to continue.

Footnotes to Chapter 2

1. For a neoclassical review of mainstream theories of wage and employment determination, see Rees (1979). For further developments of the points I make in criticism of that perspective (on its own terms), see Gordon (1972, Chapter 3).

2. There is remarkably little mainstream discussion of the supply of "good jobs" since few would recognize the legitimacy or the importance of the distinction between "good" and "poor" jobs in the first place. As a result, this inferential discussion of the logic of their analysis depends largely on my own application of the general discussion. For some essentially similar applications of the mainstream perspective to at least one employment problem, see Feldstein (1975).

3. For a general review of some of the principles upon which this kind of structural analysis builds, see Gordon (1972, Chapters 4-5) and Piore (1979).

4. The "segmentation" approach is developed in the following sources: Gordon (1972); Edwards, Reich, and Gordon (1975); Doeringer and Piore (1971); Piore (1975); and Gordon, Edwards, and Reich (1980). For surveys of some of the empirical evidence which supports the segmentation perspective, see Harrison and Sum (1978); Edwards (1979, Chapter 9); and Gordon (1980a).

5. This structural approach to regional development is developed in Alcaly and Mermelstein (1977); Tabb and Sawyers (1978); and Watkins and Perry (1979). For some supporting evidence, see Harrison and Hill (1978) and Watkins and Perry (1979).

6. Many of the basic points upon which this section relies are developed in Piore (1979) and Union for Radical Political Economics (1978).

7. Kieschnick (1979) reports data indicating that small businesses earn relatively high rates of profit in any given year. He presents those data in an effort to criticize the performance and the inefficiencies of larger firms. His argument is not inconsistent with the argument I am making in these sections. If we look at short-term rates of profit, many entrepreneurial firms, no matter how small, earn relatively high rates of profit for a time. Eventually, however, they either over-extend themselves and decline or are bought up by larger companies. Over the longer term, as Edwards (1979) shows and as I summarize the data above, large firms in concentrated industries are the only firms which achieve and sustain above-average rates of profit. As the data from Birch (1979) show—see the discussion in subsequent paragraphs in the text—small firms grow for short spurts and then decline. Their growth is often founded upon the low quality of the jobs they provide and the low wages they pay. Small firms in highly competitive industries, I conclude, cannot sustain much higher quality employment for long without structural changes in the conditions within which they operate.

8. For evidence on the association between small enterprises and secondary jobs, see Bluestone (1978); Bluestone, Murphy, and Stevenson (1973); and Harrison and Sum (1978).

3

TOWARD A
"GOOD JOBS" POLICY

Many State policymakers favor a traditional "economic development strategy" not only because they think it will work, but also because they see no clear—and practical—alternative. In this chapter I outline two alternative approaches to the provision of more "good jobs"— what I call the "traditional" and the "community" approaches. I argue further that the "traditional" approach offers little promise of moderating State employment problems, while the "community" approach, however much it flies against the tradition of State economic development policy, holds a strong potential for helping provide more "good jobs" for workers throughout the country.

ALTERNATIVE POLICY APPROACHES This section briefly defines two alternative approaches to State economic development in general and to State employment problems in particular. It links those two approaches with the two main analytic perspectives on the sources of State employment problems discussed in the previous chapter.

The current and prevalent "economic development strategy" applies what can be called a "traditional" approach to economic problems. When something needs to be done, it seeks to develop policy instruments which will make it increasingly profitable for businesses to move in the directions desired by State policymakers. If the State wants more workers hired by businesses, then it will provide something like wage subsidies to firms to encourage them to substitute labor for capital. If it wants to encourage more business activity within its own boundaries, then it will seek to reduce some or all of the relative costs of doing business in that State in order to make the local economic environment more attractive to businesses.

The "traditional" approach relies on the simple assumption that States can accomplish their economic objectives by relying on the profit maximization of private sector firms. It presumes that it is possible to induce firm activities by shifting the relative profitability of different kinds of activities. It seeks *indirectly* to achieve an ultimate objective—moderating State economic or employment problems—

60

through policies which *directly* affect business costs and profits but do *not* directly affect workers' earnings, employment security, working conditions, or job control.[1]

The "traditional" approach assumes that firms will respond to policies which affect their relative costs and profitability in ways which ultimately benefit workers and ultimately lead to the desired employment objectives. This assumption depends on mainstream economic analysis in two important ways.

First, mainstream economic analysis, as we have already seen, assumes that any changes in the environment affecting firm costs will stimulate changes in firm activities. This reflects the presumption of continuous substitution at the margin—that any change will matter— and the assumption of equilibrium—that since firms had *already* made all previous necessary adjustments to changes in their environment, current shifts in their related costs will have clear and predictable

Photo: Earl Dotter/ALEC

effects. If one argued, in contrast, that many changes in the economic environment are not large enough to affect firm decisions and/or that firms are currently preoccupied with much more important adjustments, then the presumptions of the "traditional" approach would not appear to provide promising policy guides.

Second, mainstream analysis asserts that private sector activities based on profit-seeking individual firm decisions will always come closer to achieving desired social outcomes than any other kind of economic practice. The mainstream perspective argues that private businesses always tend toward efficient operations and therefore that everyone is likely to be better off, pending appropriate compensation for externalities and diseconomies, than from other approaches. But if we began to conclude that private profit-seeking business activities were either relatively inefficient or that the policies they executed in pursuit of their own profits actually conflicted with the objectives of others in the relevant communities, then States' *a priori* preferences for the "traditional" approach might also seem misplaced.

A "community" approach to State economic policy can be defined as one which seeks to promote community objectives *directly* through the development of community mechanisms for achieving those objectives without the constraint that profit-making businesses provide the medium for achieving such objectives. A "community" approach would seek to accomplish its objectives by acting directly toward those objectives, not by relying on businesses indirectly to accomplish them for the community. (I deliberately use the term "community," rather than "public" or "government," in order to emphasize the possibility and potential desjrability of *private* non-profit mechanisms, rather than exclusively government, much less State or federal, control of such activities.) This approach does not seek opposition against small business as such. Rather, it proposes to pursue policy objectives directly, rather than pursuing them through the support of profits. If people currently operating small businesses could organize their activities in a way which directly supported articulated social objectives, they would benefit from the "community approach." What matters are the outcomes of policies, not the names of the organizations which help pursue them.

What might be the mechanisms through which a "community" approach would be applied? Pending further detail in Chapter 4, we can imagine a wide variety of possible mechanisms: government programs directly controlled by local or State governments; special community-elected boards controlling specific projects; producers or consumers' cooperatives aiming to accomplish specific economic objectives; or legally constituted non-profit community-based cor-

Photo: Robert Gumpert

63

porations with stipulated objectives. What matters, for the purposes of the ensuing discussion, is that such mechanisms be controlled by those for whom service is intended and that private profit not act as an intervening criterion affecting policy decisions. If the community seeks to profit from a given activity on a shared and equitable basis, then it would function as a "cooperative," with reward on the basis of need or direct contribution to desired program objectives, rather than as a private profit-making enterprise in which financial reward is determined on the basis of the previous distribution of wealth.

A preference for a "community" approach over a "traditional" approach would undoubtedly derive from some combination of two principal assumptions: (a) That "traditional" approaches will actually fail to accomplish the desired objectives; and/or (b) that it would make more sense to adopt policies which move *directly* toward accomplishing a set of objectives without also requiring that some public monies enrich private individuals through direct support of private profit.

The analysis developed in the preceding chapter would tend to support both of those assumptions.

■ Pro-business policies aimed at enlarging the quantity of "good jobs" available in the U.S. economy are likely to fail because the structure of the private economy makes it highly unlikely that private firms can or will provide more "good jobs."

■ Large corporations have sufficient economic dominance in the private economy that, if policymakers rely on them for accomplishing public objectives, those private corporations will exact a relatively high price in the form of substantial public support for their profits.

While the structural analysis developed in the preceding chapter suggests that the "traditional" approach has little promise and that corporations are likely to demand high returns for their cooperation with public objectives, it does not speak directly to the potential promise or effectiveness of "community" approaches themselves. The remainder of this chapter reviews some empirical evidence on the actual failures and ineffectiveness of "traditional" policy approaches in the recent past, and raises some arguments about the potential effectiveness of "community" approaches to improving the quantity of "good jobs."

DO "TRADITIONAL" APPROACHES ACTUALLY FAIL?

As most States have pursued an "economic development strategy," embodying the "traditional" approach, for many years, we have ample evidence by which to test its relative effectiveness. I shall review evidence of one major strand of the "traditional" approach in order to provide the basis for further evaluation of the claim that this approach holds little promise.

Almost universally in recent years (as noted in the introduction), States and localities have sought to attract (or retain) businesses through special tax subsidies or breaks for business activity. The underlying assumption in those policies is that a shift toward relatively lower business taxes in a particular jurisdiction will make that location relatively more attractive for firms and that, on average, the rate of growth of business activity in that jurisdiction will increase.

There is no evidence that this strategy works. Indeed, there is substantial evidence that it is destined to fail. All available empirical evidence suggests that jurisdictional tax favors for business are unlikely to have any significant effect on the rate of business activity in that jurisdiction.

Roger Vaughan, in a companion volume in this series (Vaughan, 1979), reviews the issues embodied in state tax policy in some detail. As a result, a brief summary of available evidence is sufficient.

■ "There is little evidence that overall tax levels are too high" (Vaughan, 1979). The average U.S. business pays less than one percent of its total revenues in general business taxes.

■ "Counter to many myths, tax differences can be blamed for very little of the regional shifts in employment and for relatively little of the shifts from central cities to suburbs" (Vaughan, 1979). There are several reasons for this. State and local taxes are offset against federal taxes. Tax rates are low to begin with, so that variations have slight overall effect on business activity. More important, the costs of most other factors affecting business activity swamp the influence of variations in taxes. In short, as Vaughan concludes, "the overwhelming evidence from many studies of industrial location decisions suggests that firms select their region based upon broad criteria . . . Compared with these factors, state and local taxes shrink in importance . . . . The near unanimity of findings from all sources gives some credibility to the basic proposition that tax rates have not been important."

An extended discussion by Harrison and Kanter (1978) provides similar conclusions about the broader range of business incentives **65**

Photo: Earl Dotter/ALEC

which State governments have applied: "Our research indicates that neither conventional economic theory nor . . . empirical evidence provide much support for the popular belief that states can significantly affect industrial expansion, relocation or start-up with the kind of incremental incentives they have been using." But if these incentives have so little effect, why do States keep providing them? Harrison and Kanter suggest that businesses have taken advantage of current economic insecurity by seeking tax advantages which are insignificant in the context of their overall profitability. They quote one lobbyist, perhaps more candid than others, who suggested that while businesses would prefer an absolute reduction in corporate income taxes, "tax incentives will have to do."

There is no empirical basis for believing that significant variations in state tax incentives or corporate tax levels exert much influence on business locational behavior, improve the supply of "good jobs" in a State, or offset the opportunity costs of State revenues foregone. Many policymakers will find this counter-intuitive. Aren't favors to business, leading to reductions in their costs, bound to make at least some difference?

Based on the discussion in the preceding chapter, it should now be reasonably clear why these kinds of "traditional" approaches have so little effect.

There are substantial structural rigidities in the U.S. economy. Historically, major business decisions about regional location have flowed from basic shifts in the factors affecting control over their markets and workforces. Substantial shifts in the quality of infrastructure have followed from those major business shifts. State governments would be able to counter the effects of those structural changes only if they were able to mount policies with comparable structural effects.

Are there some policy options which would have such effects and nonetheless remain consistent with the "traditional" approach?

One set of policies which might eventually influence business locational behavior would involve efforts to affect the *quality of infrastructure* in a given State. Private businesses themselves prefer not to spend money on infrastructural investment simply because they cannot typically monopolize the returns to those investments. So public policies affecting the quality of available infrastructure would require direct government action, not support for business activities.

But even if States did pursue such policies, there is little likelihood that private firms would provide any greater quantities of "good jobs" merely because the quality of the supporting infrastructure had improved. Until one had transformed the competitiveness of some   *67* firms' environments, millions of enterprises will be incapable of providing "good jobs." And until one directly affects the way in which large corporations organize production, it is unlikely that a better infrastructure would make them any more liable to increase the number of "good jobs" they make available at any given level of production or investment.

There is one other set of "traditional" policies which States could pursue which might potentially affect business location decisions. In Chapter 2, I argued that critical turning points in the dynamics of urban and regional development in the U.S. have flowed from corporate efforts to escape from areas where workers began to increase their relative strength and ability to affect the quality of their work. A variety of studies have shown, for example, that the lower wages of workers in the South primarily reflect their weaker bargaining position, not their lower skills or the particular composition of industry which has located in the South (see, for instance, Malizia, 1976). This suggests that Frostbelt States might conceivably influence firms' location decisions, over the long run, if they both modernized the infrastructure in the Frostbelt *and* dramatically reduced workers' bargaining power—supporting right-to-work laws, or firms' efforts to decertify collective bargaining units, or business assaults on minimum wage laws, or corporate evasion of the statutory intentions of the National Labor Relations Act. Business attitudes about location in the Northeast and North Central regions might be influenced, in short, if States sided much more openly and consistently with firms against workers and unions. Even here, small changes in policy would not be enough; presumably, unions would have to be pushed back to the quanitative and qualitative levels of power and influence which currently characterize both the Sunbelt and, more dramatically, countries like South Korea and Brazil to which large corporations have recently been attracted.

Were State policymakers to move in this direction, the terms of policy objectives would be altered significantly. It would no longer be true that States were pursuing the policy objectives of increasing the supply of "good jobs." Given the character of recent corporate shifts to the Sunbelt and overseas, this kind of policy approach would mean that States were explicitly seeking to support corporate profits *at the expense of the quality of work available to workers.* It seems impossible to argue, in any rigorous or coherent way, that State policies which attracted businesses because they achieved sufficient reductions in workers' power were actually serving the objectives of increasing the supply of "good jobs" in those States.

This discussion helps clarify, in the end, the specific themes which

Photo: Earl Dotter/ALEC

have recurred throughout this essay. The "traditional" approach to moderating State employment problems cannot work for either or both of two reasons. First, most State policy tools which pursue employment objectives through effects on business profits are incapable of affecting the structural characteristics of the economy which create the scarcity of "good jobs" in the first place—either by permitting peripheral firms to provide good jobs or by convincing large firms to change their employment policies. Second, those few State policies which might actually influence the behavior of large corporations would explicitly attack the quality of work and eventually reduce the supply of "good jobs" available in the economy. The structure of the economy, in short, creates conflicts between the level of business profits and the quantity of "good jobs." The "traditional" approach will either have no effects on firms' employment behavior (and provide marginal subsidies to business profits) or will have dramatic effect on business activity at the direct expense of work quality. Those who retain their concern with the quality of work and the supply of "good jobs," this argument suggests, must begin to consider alternative policy approaches.

CAN "COMMUNITY" APPROACHES ACTUALLY SUCCEED?

A "community" approach to State employment problems would seek to develop, encourage, and support non-profit, community-based mechanisms for providing "good jobs."[2] As the preceding discussion has argued, States would presumably move in these directions precisely because they offered a better chance of increasing the supply of "good jobs" than support of profit-seeking business enterprises would afford.

Can such a "community" approach work? Since there is so little non-profit, community-based enterprise at present, how can we be confident that such organizations could, in fact, overcome some of the structural problems constraining profit-seeking enterprises? How likely is it that a "community" approach could actually help moderate State employment problems by increasing the number of "good jobs" available in the economy?

In order to answer this question we need to return to basics. Any enterprise faces six necessary conditions for the effective provision of a good or service. It must be able to gain access to and effectively combine: (a) raw materials (through an available infrastructure); (b) workers in sufficient quantity with required skills; (c) appropriate production technology; (d) administrative and coordinative capacity; (e) the capital funds necessary to generate and sustain the enterprise; and (f) a demand for its output.

None of these requirements constitutes an intrinsically insuperable obstacle to a "community" approach to State employment problems. Indeed, each could be met through a concerted and coordinated public effort to pursue the "community" approach.

■ *Raw Materials and Infrastructure.* At first blush, there is obviously some grounds for concern about the provisioning of community-based enterprises. Can we assume that such enterprises will be able to gain access to energy, buildings, transportation, and other supplies at relatively "competitive" prices—regardless of the location of the communities in which they are operated? Communities in many older cities in the Frostbelt undoubtedly suffer current disadvantages in many of these respects. But this problem can be turned on its head with some careful analysis of the character of those current disadvantages.

One of the major issues currently facing economic policymakers involves infrastructural investment over the next 25 years. What kind of energy system will be developed? Will the truck continue as the dominant form of freight transport? Will industry continue to rely on electrical power as heavily has it has since 1900? Answers to these kinds of locational and infrastructural questions have been shaped in the past by an underlying corporate concern with control of employees. If a "community" approach were to acquire a dominant influence over infrastructural policymaking, in contrast, it is certainly possible that major decisions about energy, transit, and building structures themselves could be framed by a concern with the consistency of those new infrastructural investments with evenly distributed community development priorities. If decentralized solar heating helps promote decentralized manufacturing (which in turn helps provide many more "good jobs"), for example, then that becomes one important argument in fàvor of intensive technological support for solar alternatives within the framework of the community approach. If renewal of an urban rail network is both economically feasible and consistent with community-based development priorities, to pick another illustration, then that would constitute an important, relatively independent argument for intensive support for renewal of rail networks. In general, since public subsidy of an investment in infrastructure is going to be taking place over the next 25 years anyway, we stand at a crossroad of critical decisions: does infrastructural investment continue to support the advantages of large corporations and other profit-seeking enterprises, or is it fashioned increasingly out of a concern with the potential for non-profit community-based enterprises? If States (and other levels of government) fail to move in the latter directions now, then it is likely that we shall face the prospect of a private sector which provides even fewer "good jobs" in the year 2000 than it does now.

■ *Workers.* The discussion in Chapter 2 certainly indicates that there are more than enough available workers to provide a supply of labor to community-based enterprises. (Indeed, the excess supply of workers in the current economy is precisely the problem.) Moreover, the discussion in Chapter 2 seems to indicate that there is no intrinsic problem posed by the distribution of skills among workers currently available. It is certainly true that those who presently suffer the worst problems of unemployment and underemployment have relatively fewer skills than those with the best jobs. But it is equally true that the skills required for many primary jobs in the current economy can be easily learned or acquired in a very short period of time. It is also true that many workers generally confined to secondary employment are "over-qualified" for those jobs. Experience with corporate training programs of the late 1960s seems to indicate, finally, that people acquire skills quickly if they fulfill the requirements of a "good job" which is clearly available and more or less guaranteed for the trainee. In these respects, therefore, we can safely assume that community-based enterprises would be able to attract and/or train workers with **71** the skills necessary to perform tasks defined by the "good jobs" created in those enterprises.

■ *Appropriate Production Technology.* There is nothing about advanced technology as such which precludes its use by community-based enterprises or its consistency with "good jobs." Coal-mining is a very dangerous activity in the United States, for example, but that reflects the failure of U.S. mining companies to make adequate use of existing technology, not from the character of the work; the miner's job is a much "better" job in Europe than the U.S. precisely because European mines use more modern and safer technology. This example suggests an obvious conclusion: technologies can support "good job" creation as much as they can undercut it—depending on the policies and priorities which frame the exploration and utilization of technology. Non-profit, community-based enterprises would need access to modern technology, but, as long as we assume that there is nothing about advanced technology which intrinsically constrains the provision of "good jobs," then the only barrier which community-based enterprises would have to overcome would be financial, not technological. Such enterprises would need to be able to afford advanced technology, in short, but would not face "technical" obstacles to their efforts to combine effective and relatively inexpensive production with "good jobs."

■ *Administrative and Coordinative Capacity.* One impression that many policymakers have developed about community-based enterprises is that they lack administrative and coordinative capacity. There is undoubtedly some truth in these generalizations about past experience. But the issue is like those we have already discussed for infrastructure and technology. As long as the federal government and energy companies devote almost no research and development to solar technologies, for example, the available set of solar techniques will undoubtedly seem insubstantial compared to the apparent wizardry behind synthetic fuels. In the same way, the administrative skills of many fledgling community-based enterprises will pale in comparison with the technical competence of large corporations until those community enterprises receive substantial commitments of development and capital funding. Once these enterprises began to acquire a future, there would be substantial reservoirs of people with critical administrative and professional skills who would be prepared to devote energy and effort to non-profit, community-based enterprises. (The only logical ground for doubting their availability would be the tenuous assumption that professional workers would *always* refuse to apply their skills except in situations where they could assume the potential rewards of salaries in the range of $60,000-$100,000 a year.

While this is undoubtedly true of many professionals, it is undoubtedly not true of many others.) We can take the availability of these resources for granted once community-based enterprises appear to get public and private commitments of support.

■ *Capital Funds.* Non-profit community-based enterprises would also require access to substantial capital funds in order to be able to develop effective, cost-efficient systems for producing goods and services which people need in ways which maximize their abilities to provide "good jobs" for those who need them. Would State governments have to pour substantial subsidies into the reduction of the net costs of capital acquisition in order to create some space in the sun for small enterprises?

In their detailed study in a companion volume in this series, Litvak and Daniels (1979) argue that while variations in the *cost* of capital are fairly unimportant to the success or viability of business enterprises, simple *access* to capital is critical for such success. They conclude, "the key point, then, is not subsidizing the cost of capital, but ensuring its availability for profitable enterprise."

Where could such capital come from? Would State governments have to put up the money themselves? Would this therefore drain public tax coffers or strain governments' current bonding capacity?

There are vast capital resources in this country whose current allocation is nominally regulated by State (and, to some extent, federal) governments. These funds include public and private pension funds, savings bank deposits, and insurance company assets. In each of these three cases, people have amassed savings which have been placed in the hands of the executors of those savings—trust or fund managers, banks, and insurance companies. The government establishes the regulatory framework under which the managers of those funds must operate. Current government policy allows such managers to allocate those investment funds however they wish to whomever they choose—subject to basic regulations on mismanagement and cost effectiveness. But there is no reason why local and State governments could not choose to stipulate a range of activities which deserve investment priority and a boundary to the geographic area in which such funds might be allocated. Such a precedent has been established recently in some anti-redlining legislation, which requires, in effect, that a stipulated percentage of savings bank deposits (say, 25 percent) be allocated for investment (in home mortgages, for example). These precedents could be applied to pension funds and insurance company assets with exactly the same logic as with savings deposits. The point seems clear: If people amass savings, why shouldn't those savings be channeled in directions which best serve the interests of people in their own communities, not the interests of people somewhere else? And why shouldn't people's local and State governments become involved in establishing criteria for such investment regulation?

Free market advocates typically reply that savers want the highest possible rate of return for their savings, that they would not be prepared to make a sacrifice of potential interest and equity accumulation for the sake of the "community interest." But this assumes that profit-seeking enterprises are always capable of paying a higher rate of return on assets invested than non-profit community-based enterprises. Much of the argument to this point should have raised serious doubts about the tenability of that assumption. Investments in small profit-seeking enterprises, as we can see from the Birch data reviewed at the end of Chapter 2, are bound to seem shaky—as Birch puts it, a "banker's nightmare." Investments in large corporations are more reliable, but large corporations must cover profits and dividends which non-profit, community-based enterprises would not need to cover. It is certainly plausible that community-based enterprises, with appropriate access to capital funding and government backing in the short run, would be able to reduce their costs of business per unit of output to levels at least comparable with those of large private firms and that they would therefore be able to pay comparable rates of return on investment.

Thus, a strong argument can be made for the potential viability of non-profit, community-based enterprises *if* governments provide initial support and backing and *if* governments pursue regulatory policies which seek to channel available capital in directions which make sense from the point of view of the general public. The federal government is considering such intervention on behalf of large private corporations—with possible loan guarantees to companies like Chrysler and billions of dollars of technical development to support projects like synthetic fuels which private companies will eventually control. Why shouldn't State governments consider alternative policies of comparable scope in directions which hold much greater promise of "good job" generation?

■ *Product Demand.* Having proceeded this far, the last step seems easy. If we can assume that non-profit, community-based enterprises would receive sufficient public support to solve the other problems they would face, then they could presumably produce goods and services which people need and would buy. Consumers in this country would clearly buy food if it were of higher quality and/or at lower cost than that currently provided by large food processors and chains. People obviously need decent low-cost housing. People desperately need better, less expensive, and more reliable health care. There is a crying need for conservation projects and reliable low-cost energy. Millions need alternative forms of transportation. And millions need services like education and counseling which would help them pursue their other objectives. If community-based enterprises developed the capacity to produce these kinds of high quality goods and services at relatively low cost, the problems of product demand could easily be solved.

Although the preceding paragraphs suggest that there are no *intrinsic* barriers to the development of viable, non-profit community-based enterprises, two further, much more general issues need to be addressed—one at what economists would call the *micro-economic* level and one at the *macro-economic* level.

Is it actually possible that community-based enterprises could compete with and provide equally cost-effective goods and services as profit-seeking private enterprises? Doesn't the "free market" guarantee efficiency? Three points seem important about the micro-economics of this comparison.

First, all large corporations receive and rely on government support; there is no such thing as a pure "free market" in this respect. Large corporations rely on public subsidies for infrastructure and research and development. They have come to expect bail-outs and guarantees. They demand and receive investment tax credits, accelerated depreciation allowances, and support for product demand. Indeed, it is reasonable to argue that even the largest of private corporations, like General Motors and Ford (much less Chrysler), would not be able to operate as they currently do without having received critical public support and subsidy over the years. Isn't it possible that comparable commitments of public resources and support to community-based enterprises would make more sense?

Second, even with all that support, profit-seeking enterprises are not necessarily "efficient." They spend billions on administrative costs necessary to control world markets which much smaller, community-based enterprises would not need to spend. They spend billions on huge salaries for their chief executive personnel. They spend billions on advertising designed to convince consumers to purchase products of questionable quality. All of these expenditures are built into the costs and therefore the prices of the goods of those corporations. They rarely face the competition of enterprises which do not incur those costs because neither the private nor the public sector has ever devoted resources and capital to the development of such non-profit corporations.

Third, community-based enterprises would presumably face some   **75** disciplinary pressures of their own which would constrain potential waste. Theory tells us that product-market competition and investors' thirst for profits keep profit-seeking firms honest. Theory would also suggest that consumers' demand for quality (for their money) and community-based political and investment controls would presumably have equivalent effects on non-profit, community-based enterprises. Just as some profit-seeking firms engage in corrupt and inefficient practices, disproving the perfect reliability of the theory of the "free market," so has it turned out that some "community-based" and private organizations have not behaved perfectly either. In theory, nonetheless, there is every reason to expect that a concerted movement toward the "community" approach would develop continuing pressures on non-profit, community-based enterprises to remain efficient and effective.

In short, one cannot predict, *a priori,* the greater efficiency of profit-seeking over non-profit, community-based enterprises. If that is true at the micro-economic level, then the likelihood that non-profit, community-based enterprises would provide "good jobs" more reliably than their private, profit-seeking counterparts seems, by itself, to establish a sufficient rationale for devoting State government policy toward their creation and support.

What about macro-economics? Doesn't the current priority on fighting inflation rule out expanded public commitment to new kinds of policies and activities?

When we look closely at such concerns, it turns out that exactly the opposite kind of conclusion seems more appropriate: Movement toward policies which would seek "good job" generation through non-profit, community-based enterprises would also make important contributions toward the moderation of some of our principal current macro-economic problems. This is not the place to review the sources of those macro-economic problems at length, but two points seem crucial.

First, productivity has stagnated and unemployment remains high *not* because corporations lack profits and capital funds—since corporate profits have recently soared—but because corporations have been reluctant to invest (at least in this country) because of concern for the basic instability of the political and economic climate in the United States. If State governments began to pursue policies that would help "stabilize" the process of investment and employment growth, then some of the current instability would potentially be reduced. Public support for "good job" generation should also help restimulate private investment and demand.

Second, the development of non-profit, community-based enterprises would help improve the terms of the trade-off between inflation and unemployment. On the employment side, these enterprises would probably generate more jobs per unit of output and investment than large private, profit-seeking enterprises: I have explored the reasons for this in previous discussion. On the price side, they would probably reduce the rate of inflation associated with any given level of output: If we assumed that consumer demand was at a particular level, and that there was a shift toward production by non-profit, community-based enterprises, then production costs at that given level of output might be lower than under present circumstances because fewer resources would be devoted to relatively unproductive corporate expenses like high executive salaries and expensive advertising.

But this immediately raises a final macro-economic question: If increasing support for non-profit, community-based enterprises generated more good jobs, would this not, by definition, increase average wage levels; therefore increase aggregate labor costs; and, consequently, increase prices through cost mark-up pricing? There are two reasons why the "community" approach would not necessarily have those hypothetical effects on prices.

First, some of the increased wage costs would come out of what *currently* goes toward corporate profits. Second, and perhaps more important, the increasing costs for wages paid to workers with "good jobs" could potentially come out of what now covers the salaries of high-paid executives and professionals. Let us assume that there are now about 750,000 salaried workers who earn more than $75,000 a year. (The government does not release separate data on people earning more than $50,000 a year, but this "guesstimate" is relatively conservative.) Their salaries, by themselves, would be enough to cover the wages of nearly four million workers earning $15,000 a year at full-time, year-round employment—accounting for a huge share of those who currently lose working hours to unemployment during a given year. However hypothetical, these calculations suggest an obvious point: If there were a shift toward production in enterprises devoted to providing "good jobs," and if that movement effectively generated an aggregate shift toward a more equal distribution of labor incomes among wage-and-salary employees, then higher wages for those not now in good jobs would not necessarily add to production costs.

Suppose that there were a dramatic policy shift toward the "community" approach? What would happen to the rest of the economy? Would there be a collapse elsewhere?

There is no doubt that a movement in the directions identified by the "community" approach would involve substantial shifts in the character of economic activity in the United States. But it would not involve any necessary attack on the right of private businesses to operate. Private, profit-making businesses would simply face additional and more stringent competitive pressures. If they wanted access to certain pools of capital, they would have to meet the standards by which that capital was allocated. Meeting those standards, they would be able to go about their businesses.

This does not amount to a policy position which opposes business profits just to oppose business profits. It builds from an argument that other social objectives, like the quest for better jobs, deserve higher priority than profits. Where support for profits and support for "good jobs" conflict, support for profits should take second place. If no conflicts exist between those policy objectives, so much the better.

In conclusion, a "community" approach to the generation of "good jobs" is both plausible and desirable. One important topic remains for further discussion. In Chapter 4, I turn to a brief discussion of the policy instruments which one might apply in moving toward a "community" approach to State employment problems.

Footnotes to Chapter 3

1. There is no slackening in mainstream economists' support for this "traditional" approach. The National Commission for Manpower Policy recently released a special report on "Increasing Job Opportunities in the Private Sector." In the introduction, Eli Ginzberg, who has long argued the importance of greater attention to the problems of "good jobs" and "poor jobs," adopts a simple position about current policy directions: "If the enlarged participation of the private sector in federal training and employment programs is a sound objective—and it is difficult to argue otherwise—then tax as well as a range of other devices that might elicit a positive response from the business community are worth exploring." (National Commission for Manpower Policy, 1978: 5.)

2. This "community" approach has not yet been well-developed in great detail, but similar discussions with somewhat more institutional detail and concrete discussion of proposals are available in Rifkin and Barber (1978); Faux and Lightfoot (1976); Case, Goldberg and Shearer (1976); and Conference on Alternative State and Local Policies (1977).

4

POLICY TOOLS FOR
DIFFERENT SEASONS

For policymaking purposes, it is obviously insufficient to leave off our analysis with only a sketch of general approaches to employment policy. In this very brief chapter I highlight the implications of the preceding analysis for specific choices among policy instruments aimed at moderating State employment problems, and attempt to exemplify the basic differences between the "traditional" approach and the "community" approach to "good job" creation. I do this in order to show that the specific choice of policy instrument matters much *less* than the basic approach to "good job" creation which State policymakers pursue: Any given policy instrument offers little promise if applied within the framework of the "traditional" approach to moderating State employment problems; but the very same instruments could be employed with more promise in the context of a "community" approach to "good job" creation.

Because the purpose of this chapter is to illustrate an argument rather than to develop a complete and exhaustive menu of policy options, I have chosen a relatively limited set of examples as a basis for the development of this argument.

Skills Training Many public agencies continue to promote skills training programs as a solution to employment problems. When skeptics cite evidence of the occasional failures of previous efforts in these directions, skills training proponents respond with innovative twists on the traditional models, arguing that slightly more ingenious programs will have demonstrably more favorable results. This kind of discussion largely misses the most important issue: The promise of skills training depends entirely on the *context* in which the training takes place.

On the one hand, skills training programs aimed at jobs in the private sector are unlikely to have any significant effect on the supply of "good jobs" provided by the private sector. Small firms in competitive industries do not currently provide many jobs requiring substantial skills. Increasing reliance on skilled workers, in the case of these enterprises, would require sufficient market stability and capital funding to permit changes in the character of their production process. **79**

Skills training by itself does not address the basic obstacles to "good job" creation in small competitive firms.

In contrast, large firms can afford to hire skilled workers but prefer, other things equal, to reduce their reliance on skilled workers. As I pointed out in Chapter 2, the internal job structures of large firms are so rigid and inflexible that an increased supply of skilled workers—or a public subsidy of training costs—is highly unlikely to increase their inclination to use more skilled workers or provide more good jobs. (The example of the boatyard's calculus on welding costs discussed in Chapter 2 illustrates this kind of rigidity, even though it refers to a somewhat different kind of specific problem.) To the extent that this is true, then public subsidy of training costs for workers who are eventually hired by large firms has the effect *not* of increasing the number of "good jobs" which those firms provide *but rather* of increasing their profits as a result of the reduction in their internal costs of training. This leads, in the end, to public tax subsidy of corporate profits. If we assume that those tax dollars could otherwise help support programs which would help generate "good jobs," we confront once again the apparent conflict between private profit and the supply of "good jobs."

On the other hand, skills training would make considerable sense if pursued in the context of a "community" approach to "good job" creation. While there is a large supply of workers with skills available

Photo: Robert Gumpert

in the labor market as a whole, there are also many workers whose education and employment experience have not provided them with many productive skills. The corporate experiments of the late 1960s, as Cohn (1971) shows, demonstrated that workers from "disadvantaged" backgrounds could and would acquire skills training rapidly if they were convinced that a "good job" awaited them at the end of the training road. Skills training would enhance the "community" approach to "good job" generation for those who need skills development. The costs of skills training, in the long run, would certainly be outweighed by the reduced costs of unemployment insurance, welfare benefits, and crime prevention to which the current policy failures to reduce unemployment rates now contribute.

Tax Incentives and Investment Subsidies

Tax subsidies and investment incentives, by themselves, are unlikely to affect the supply of good jobs. (See Kieschnick, 1979; and the Advisory Commission on Intergovernmental Relations, 1978, for further discussion on these general points.) Indeed, the wide variety of tax incentives and investment subsidies all have the same intended effect. They hope to reduce the costs of business operations along certain dimensions—such as inducing more investment or attracting business to a particular location. But these policies are unlikely to affect firms' behavior at the margin. Structural changes would be necessary in order either to make possible small firms' provision of "good jobs" or to guarantee that large firms would move toward the provision of more (rather than fewer) "good jobs." Without those structural changes, tax incentives and investment subsidies are unlikely to change the structure of employment which private, profit-seeking firms provide and are likely, instead, to subsidize profits, at any given level of economic activity, at the expense of taxpayers' spendable earnings.

In contrast, the equivalent of such tax subsidies and investment incentives might have dramatic effects in the context of a sustained community approach to "good job" creation. Suppose that State governments began to develop infrastructure and other coordinated policies to develop and support non-profit, community-based enterprises (as opposed to such current support of large corporations). Tax incentives and investment subsidies (at levels more or less equivalent to current "tax expenditures" to large private corporations) might then help provide critical support for new community-based enterprises during those early periods of incubation when they "shake out" their problems and try to develop the size of operations which permits decent economies of scale. The point is that such subsidies would be part of an explicit public effort to use government policy instruments to promote "good job" creation (among other policy objectives), not simply to provide inducements to private profit-seeking corporations to undertake whatever investments they prefer regardless of the impact of those investments on State employment problems.

The Government as Employer of Last Report

Many have sought, through their support for policy initiatives like the Humphrey-Hawkins Bill or CETA appropriations, to enlist the government as the "employer of last resort" when those desiring work have not been able to find adequate employment in the private sector. Once again, this policy fails to discriminate between the implications of a "traditional" and a "community" approach to employment problems.

If the government functions as an employer of last resort without undertaking other policies to provide capital and administrative support for the labor activities of the workers it hires under such programs, it virtually condemns those workers to jobs which pay low wages and offer insecure futures. Almost by definition, these government programs seek no other productive resources with which "employees of last resort" can work. This means that they may be able to rake leaves but that they cannot easily produce decent housing for those who need it. This means, in turn, that such workers cannot easily command the kind of pay and employment security which would justify the wages required by our definition of "good jobs." Indeed, the very definition of employment of last resort suggests that workers will be laid off as soon as the government decides that employment conditions in the private sector will accommodate those currently employed in those public jobs. (And the presumption that the public sector should not compete with the private sector, leading to no resource funding to support the productiveness of "employees of last resort," inevitably relegates such employees to relatively inefficient activities.) This approach almost explicitly consigns the "last hired" by the private sector to alternating periods of private and public employment, exposing them to bouts of intermittent unemployment, and denying them the opportunity to develop some of the skills and experience which continuing and stable employment might alternatively provide.

In contrast, public employment in the service of a "community" approach to "good job" creation could have important additive effects. Suppose the government hires people to develop plans for community-based enterprises (which would emphasize the provision

82

of "good jobs"). Suppose that these employees got the inside track to jobs in those community-based enterprises once they developed a firm foundation. This would mean that government expenditures on current employment would potentially lead to permanent and adequate employment of those employees in the private, non-profit, community-based sector. This approach would not only increase the chances of permanent employment for those whom the government currently employs but would also promise declining government expenditures on "employment of last resort" over time. The difference between government employment in this context and government employment as a residual in a "traditional" approach is that we could presume, over the long run, an increasing supply of "good jobs" from community-based enterprises, whereas we cannot presume such an increase from private sector economic activity. The critical task, if we hope to turn government employment in these relatively more promising directions, is to link current government employment with a complex of coordinated policies aimed at the longer-term development and support of non-profit, community-based enterprises oriented toward "good job" creation.

Wage Subsidies and Employment Vouchers

Some analysts, like Vaughan (1978), have proposed increasing government concentration on programs providing wage subsidies (or employment vouchers) for firms in order to encourage a shift toward a higher utilization of labor and, ultimately, more employment.

These policies hold little promise if applied within the context of the "traditional" approach to employment problems. For small firms, wage subsidies are unlikely to overcome the obstacles to small firm generation of "good jobs." Small firms in competitive industries cannot solve the problems of infrastructure and capital access, regardless of marginal variations in the relative costs of labor they face. Even if wage subsidy programs induced a partial substitution of labor for capital at the margin, small firms would be unlikely to be able to provide the kind of employment security, decent working conditions and job control which we have also defined as necessary components of "good jobs."

The problems with wage subsidies to large firms are similar to those we earlier discussed for skills training. Because of the inflexibility of job structures, wage subsidies might not necessarily induce the substitution of labor for capital within structured internal labor markets. Nor would they be likely to affect large firms' preferences for relatively fewer "powerful" employees. Instead of inducing firms to   *83* provide more "good jobs," wage subsidies might principally have the alternative effect of using tax dollars to reduce firms' wage costs and therefore to increase their profits (with respect to internal wage expenditures). Instead of generating more good jobs, in short, wage subsidy programs would be likely to subsidize profits with public tax dollars.

In contrast, within the context of a sustained "community" approach to State employment problems, monies spent on wage subsidies might help support initial start-up costs for community-based enterprises, promoting the development of those enterprises and eventually permitting, after early incubation, a gradual reduction in their reliance on those wage subsidies. What matters, once again, is the context in which such a policy instrument is applied and the longer-term economic directions which those short-term expenditures help sustain.

Whither the "Community" Approach?

I have briefly provided some examples which indicate that the basic approach which policymakers pursue matters *more* than the specific economic activities which their policy instruments are designed to affect. Whether govern-

ments seek to affect skills training, rates of employment, or relative labor costs, the considerations which argue in favor of the "community" approach in general will also argue in favor of the application of any given policy instrument *within the context of that general policy approach.*

State policymakers should seek to apply all policy instruments currently or potentially at their disposal to full support of the "community" approach. This will require a coordinated and sustained effort to encourage, develop, and support non-profit, community-based enterprises devoted to providing growing numbers of "good jobs." Policies aimed at this direction should necessarily focus on improving these enterprises' access to (a) raw materials and infrastructure; (b) workers with adequate skills; (c) appropriate production technology; (d) adequate administrative and coordinative capacities; (e) sufficient capital funds; and (f) access to suitable demand for the goods and services they might conceivably produce. For further detail on some of the specific directions which such a coordinated policy approach might take during the 1980s, see Litvak and Daniels (1979), Coltman and Metzenbaum (1979), Philip (1978), Kieschnick (1979), and Harrison and Bluestone (1980).

This brings us to a point of conclusion.

I have argued that State governments should make dramatic changes in the direction of their policies aimed at current employment problems. I have suggested in sequence:

■ that the economy needs more "good jobs," not simply more jobs regardless of their quality;
■ that a *structural* analysis of the economy's failure to provide enough "good jobs" provides a much more adequate explanation of that failure than traditional mainstream economic analyses of job and wage determination;
■ that this structural analysis suggests the preferability and plausibility of a "community" approach to moderating State employment problems and argues against the currently prevalent "traditional" approach; and
■ that these differences in basic policy approach matter more than the specific character of particular policy instruments which government policymakers normally consider.

I have tried to develop these arguments with as much attention to logical coherence and empirical evidence as possible. I have made virtually no reference to the obvious political obstacles which would confront a sustained government effort to move in the directions indicated by the "community" approach to employment problems.

Many policymakers feel that the citizenry favors the private sector over the public sector, free enterprise over public enterprise, and corporate initiative over public initiative. But these attitudes are themselves the product of public pronouncements and prevailing policy. Many white U.S. citizens displayed obvious racial prejudice through the 19th and early 20th centuries, for example, but when public policies began to change in the 1940s, 1950s, and early 1960s, public attitudes followed closely behind.

Similar changes seem possible with employment policy. We desperately need to move toward rapid moderation of our current employment problems. The arguments of this essay suggest that this will require something like the "community" approach sketched in the preceding pages. The logic of those arguments indicates that we have no other alternative. The urgency of the problem requires that these arguments be addressed directly and openly. I have little doubt that public opinion will respond.

BIBLIOGRAPHY

Advisory Commission on Intergovernmental Relations, "Regional Growth Study," mimeographed, August 22, 1978.

Alcaly, Roger, and Mermelstein, David. *The Fiscal Crisis of American Cities.* New York: Random House, 1977.

Ashford, Nicholas. *Crisis in the Workplace: Occupational Disease and Injury.* Cambridge, Mass.: MIT, 1976.

Berg, Ivar. *Education and Jobs: The Great Training Robbery.* New York: Praeger, 1970.

Berman, Daniel M. *Death on the Job: Occupational Health and Safety Struggles in the United States.* New York: Monthly Review Press, 1979.

Bernstein, Irving. *The Turbulent Years.* Boston: Houghton-Mifflin, 1971.

Birch, David L. *The Job Generation Process.* Cambridge, Mass.: MIT Program on Neighborhood and Regional Change, 1979.

Bluestone, Barry. "The Determinants of Personal Earnings in the U.S.: Human Capital vs. Stratified Labor Markets," mimeographed, Boston College, 1978.

_____. Murphy, William M., and Stevenson, Mary. *Low Wages and the Working Poor.* Ann Arbor: University of Michigan, 1973.

Braverman, Harry. *Labor and Monopoly Capital.* New York: Monthly Review Press, 1974.

Case, John; Goldberg, Leonard; and Shearer, Derek. "State Business," *Working Papers,* Spring 1976.

Cohn, Jules, *The Conscience of the Corporations.* New York: Praeger, 1971.

Coltman, Edward; and Metzenbaum, Shelley. "Investing in Ourselves—Public Employee Pension Fund Investment: Strategies for Economic Impact and Social Responsibility." Mimeographed, Low Income Planning Aid, 2 Park Square, Boston, Mass.: June 1979.

Conference on Alternative State and Local Policies. *New Directions in State and Local Policy.* Washington, D.C.: CASLPP, 1977.

Doeringer, Peter and Piore, Michael. *Internal Labor Markets and Manpower Analysis.* Lexington, Mass.: Heath, 1971.

Edwards, Richard C. "What Makes a Good Worker? Organizational Incentives and the Determinants of Individual Earnings." *Journal of Human Resources,* October 1976.

_____. *Contested Terrain: The Transformation of the Workplace in the Twentieth Century.* New York: Basic Books, 1979.

_____. , Reich, Michael; and Gordon, David M., eds. *Labor Market Segmentation.* Lexington, Mass.: Heath, 1975.

Faux, Jeff; and Lightfoot, Robert. *Capital and Community.* Washington, D.C.: Exploratory Project for Economic Alternatives, 1976.

Feldstein, Martin. *Lowering the Permanent Rate of Unemployment.* Washington, D.C.: Joint Economic Committee, U.S. Congress, 1975.

Fogelson, Robert. *The Fragmented Metropolis.* Cambridge, Mass.: Harvard University Press, 1967.

Freeman, Richard, ed. *The Over-Educated American.* New York: Academic Press, 1976.

Ginzberg, Eli. "The Job Problem," *Scientific American,* November 1977.

Gordon, David M. *Theories of Poverty and Underemployment.* Lexington, Mass: Heath, 1972.

────. "Digging Up the Roots: The Economic Determinants of Social Problems." *Social Welfare Forum,* 1975.

────. ed. *Problems in Political Economy: An Urban Perspective.* 2nd ed. Lexington, Mass.: Heath, 1977.

────. "Capitalism and the Historical Development of American Cities." In W. Tabb and L. Sawyers, ed., *Marxism and the Metropolis.* New York: Oxford University Press, 1978.

────. "Empirical and Methodological Issues in the Theory of Labor Segmentation." In M. Reich et al., *The Segmentation of Labor in the United States.* New York: Cambridge University Press, 1980.

────. Toward the Critique of CAPITALopolis. Manuscript in Progress, 1980.

────. Edwards, Richard C.; and Reich, Michael. "The Historical Development of Labor Segmentation in the United States." In M. Reich et al., *The Segmentation of Labor in the United States.* New York: Cambridge University Press, 1980.

Greenbaum, Joan M. *In the Name of Efficiency: Management Theory and Shopfloor Practice in Data-Processing Work.* Philadelphia: Temple University Press, 1979.

Harrison, Bennett. "Education and the Secondary Labor Market." *Wharton Quarterly,* 1974.

────. "Work and Welfare." *Review of Radical Political Economics,* Fall 1979.

────. ; and Hill, Edward. "The Changing Structure of Jobs in Older and Younger Cities." In *Central City Economic Development.* Binghamton, N.Y.: Center for Social Analysis at SUNY-Binghamton, 1978.

────. and Kanter, Sandra. "The Political Economy of State Job-Creation Business Incentives." *Journal of the American Institute of Planners,* November 1978.

────. and Sum, Andrew. "Labor Market Data Requirements from the Perspective of 'Dual' or 'Segmented' Labor Market Research." Report to the National Commission on Employment and Unemployment Statistics, 1978.

────. and Bluestone, Barry. *Capital Mobility and Economic Dislocation.* Washington, D.C.: The Progressive Alliance, forthcoming, 1980.

Herbers, John. "Nationwide Revolt on Taxes Showing No Sign of Abating." *New York Times,* August 5, 1979.

Institute for Social Research. *Quality of Worklife Survey, 1977.* Ann Arbor, Mich.: Institute for Social Research, Univ. of Michigan, 1979.

Kerr, William O. "The Effects of Unionism in a Dual Labor Market." Unpublished Ph.D. Dissertation, New School for Social Research, 1979.

Kieschnick, Michael. *Small Business and Community Economic Development.* Washington, D.C.: National Center for Economic Alternatives, July 1979.

Kraft, Philip. *Programmers and Managers: The Routinization of Computer Programming in the United States.* New York: Springer-Verlag, 1977.

Levine, Robert. *The Poor Ye Need Not Have With You: Lessons from the War on Poverty.* Cambridge, Mass.: MIT Press, 1970.

Litvak, Larry and Daniels, Belden. *Innovations in Development Finance.* Washington, D.C.: Council of State Planning Agencies, 1979.

Long, Larry H., "Inter-regional Migration of the Poor: Some Recent Changes," *Current Population Reports,* Special Studies, Series P-23, Number 73, November 1978.

Luft, Harold. *Poverty and Health.* Cambridge, Mass.: Ballinger, 1978.

Malizia, Emil. "Earnings, Profits, and Productivity in North Carolina." Mimeographed, University of North Carolina, May 1976.

McGahey, Richard. "The Economics of Crime: A Critical Review of the Literature." Mimeographed, New School for Social Research, 1979.

National Advisory Council on Economic Opportunity. *Eleventh Report.* Washington, D.C.: NACEO, June 1979.

National Commission for Manpower Policy, "Increasing Job Opportunities in the Private Sector: A Conference Report." *Special Report,* No. 29, November 1978.

Nation's Business. *The Years of Change: An Almanac of American Progress.* Washington, D.C.: Chamber of Commerce, 1978.

Pack, Janet Rothenberg. "Frostbelt and Sunbelt: Convergence over Time." *Intergovernmental Perspectives,* Fall 1978.

Philip, Alan Butt. *Creating New Jobs: A Report on Long-Term Job Creation in Britain and Sweden.* London: Policy Studies Institute, 1-2 Castle Lane, London SW1E 6DR, 1978.

Piore, Michael J. "Notes Toward a Theory of Labor Market Stratification." in R.C. Edwards et al., eds., *Labor Market Segmentation.* Lexington, Mass.: Heath, 1975.

————. ed. *Unemployment and Inflation.* White Plains, N.Y.: M.E. Sharpe, 1979.

Plotnick, Robert D.; and Skidmore, Felicity. *Progress Against Poverty: A Review of the 1964-1974 Decade.* New York: Academic Press, 1975.

Rainwater, Lee. *What Money Buys.* New York: Basic Books, 1975.

Rees, Albert. *The Economics of Work and Pay.* 2nd ed. New York: Harper & Row, 1979.

Rifkin, Jeremy. *Own Your Own Job: Economic Democracy for Working Americans.* New York: Bantam Books, 1977.

————. and Barber, Randy. *The North Will Rise Again: Pensions, Politics, and Power in the 1980s.* Boston: Beacon Press, 1978.

Silk, Leonard; and Vogel, David. *Ethics and Profits: The Crisis of the American Corporation.* New York: Simon and Schuster, 1976.

Sternlieb, George, and Hughes, James, eds. Revitalizing the Northeast. New Brunswick: Center for Urban Policy Research, 1978.

Tabb, William; and Sawyers, Lawrence, eds. *Marxism and the Metropolis*. New York: Oxford University Press, 1978.

Union for Radical Political Economics, ed. *U.S. Capitalism in Crisis*. New York: Union for Radical Political Economics, 1978.

Vaughan, Roger J. "Jobs for the Urban Unemployed." Mimeographed, March 1978.

————. *State Taxation and Economic Development*. Washington, D.C.: Council of State Planning Agencies, 1979.

Watkins, Alfred; and Perry, David, eds. *The Rise of the Sunbelt Cities*. Beverly Hills, Ca.: Sage Publications, 1979.

Woods, Robert. *1400 Governments*. New York: Anchor Books, 1959.

STUDIES IN STATE DEVELOPMENT POLICY

Please send me the following publications:

Quantity	Title	No.	Price	Total
_____	*State Taxation and Economic Development*	3614	$9.95	_____
_____	*Economic Development: The Challenge of the 1980s*	3610	$9.95	_____
_____	*Innovations in Development Finance*	3612	$9.95	_____
_____	*The Working Poor*	3611	$8.95	_____
_____	*Inflation and Unemployment*	3618	$8.95	_____
_____	*Democratizing the Development Process*	3616	$7.95	_____
_____	*Venture Capital and Urban Development*	3613	$8.95	_____
_____	*Development Politics: Private Development and the Public Interest*	3617	$8.95	_____
_____	*The Capital Budget*	3615	$8.95	_____
	TOTAL ORDER			_____

☐ Payment enclosed (no charge for handling and postage)

☐ Please bill me (postage and $2 handling charge will be added)

Payment must accompany all orders under $20.

Name: _____

Title: _____

Address: _____

_____

City, State, Zip _____

Make checks payable to the Council of State Planning Agencies.

Important Note: Discounts of 10% are available on any order of four or more titles. A discount of 20% is available to individuals and institutions ordering the entire nine-volume series ($60.00 per set). Full payment must accompany requests for discounts.